THE ESSENTIAL
AMERICA

STUDY GUIDE

VOLUME II

THE ESSENTIAL AMERICA

TINDALL, SHI, and PEARCY

STUDY GUIDE

VOLUME II

CHARLES W. EAGLES

UNIVERSITY OF MISSISSIPPI

W · W · NORTON & COMPANY · NEW YORK · LONDON

Composition and layout by Roberta Flechner Graphics.

ISBN 0-393-97724-2 (pbk.)

W.W. Norton & Company, Inc.
500 Fifth Avenue, New York, N.Y. 10110
www.wwnorton.com

W. W. Norton & Company Ltd.
Castle House, 75/76 Wells St., London W1T 3QT

1 2 3 4 5 6 7 8 9 0

CONTENTS

INTRODUCTION

This *Study Guide* is designed to help you learn the basic information in *The Essential America* by George B. Tindall, David E. Shi, and Thomas Lee Pearcy. It is not intended as a replacement for the textbook but as an aid to be used along with the text. When used conscientiously, this *Study Guide* will help you to learn the essential facts of American history and to do well on quizzes based on your reading.

STRUCTURE OF THIS STUDY GUIDE

Each chapter of the *Study Guide* contains the following sections:

Chapter Objectives
Chapter Outline
Key Items of Chronology
Terms to Master
Vocabulary Building
Exercises for Understanding:
　Multiple-Choice Questions
　True-False Questions
　Essay Questions
Answers to Multiple-Choice and True-False
　Questions

The purpose of each of the sections, along with the instructions for its use, is explained below.

Chapter Objectives

For each chapter you will find about five objectives on which you should focus your atten-tion as you read. Each objective will highlight an important concept, theme, or idea in the chapter. Keep the objectives in mind while reading the whole chapter—they will help you avoid getting bogged down and missing the major points of the chapter.

Chapter Outline

Read the outline carefully before you begin reading the chapter in the textbook. Often, head-ings in the outline will suggest questions about the material. In Chapter 19, for example, the out-line entry "Labor conditions and organizations" might prompt the questions "What were the con-ditions experienced by industrial workers in the late nineteenth century?" and "What were the major labor organizations of the time?" but it might also suggest other questions such as "How did labor organizations seek to change the work-ing conditions of their members? and "How suc-cessful were the labor organizations?" Look for answers to such questions as you read the text. This approach will help students who are new to reading history.

Key Items of Chronology

Each chapter of this *Study Guide* will include a list of dates. You need not learn every date you encounter in the chapter, but if you learn the key ones listed here and any other dates emphasized by your instructor, you will have the sound chronological framework so important for understanding historical events.

Keep in mind that dates, while important, are not the sole subject matter of history. Seldom will any of the quizzes in this *Study Guide* ask for recall of dates. On the other hand, term papers and answers to essay questions should include important dates and show that you are familiar with the chronology of your subject.

Terms to Master

This section of the *Study Guide* gives you a list of important terms to study. (Remember, of course, that your instructor may emphasize additional terms that you should learn.) After reading each chapter, return to the list of terms and write a brief definition of each. If you cannot recall the term readily, turn to the relevant pages in the textbook and reread the discussion of the term. If you need or want to consult another source, go to the annotated bibliography at the end of the relevant chapter, or ask your instructor for suggestions.

Vocabulary Building

This is a section of the *Study Guide* that you may or may not need. If you do not know the meaning of the words or terms listed in Vocabulary Building, look them up in a dictionary before you begin reading the chapter. By looking up these words and then using them yourself, you will increase your vocabulary.

Exercises for Understanding

You should reserve these exercises to use as a check on your reading after you study the chapter. The multiple-choice and true-false questions included here will test your recall and understanding of the facts in the chapter. The answers to these questions are found at the end of each *Study Guide* chapter.

Essay Questions

The essay questions that come next may be used in several ways. If you are using this *Study Guide* entirely on your own, you should try to outline answers to these questions based on your reading of the chapter. In the early stages of the course you may want to consider writing formal answers to these essay questions just as you would if you encountered them on an exam. The questions will often be quite broad and will lead you to think about material in the chapter in different ways. By reviewing the essay questions in this *Study Guide* before attending class, you will better understand the class lecture or discussion.

STUDYING HISTORY

The term "history" has been defined in many ways. One way to define it is "everything that has happened in the past." But there are serious problems with this definition. First, it is simply impossible to recount *everything* that has happened in the past. Any single event is a combination of an infinite number of subevents. Each of these is itself composed of an unlimited number of subevents. The past, which includes everything that has happened, is shapeless; history is a way of lending shape to the past by focusing on significant events and their relationships.

Second, the historical record is limited. As you will discover, there is much we don't know about everyday life in nineteenth-century America. History must be based on fact and evidence. The historian then, using the evidence available, fashions a story in which certain past events are connected and take on special meaning or significance. If we accept this definition, we will recognize that much history is subjective, or influenced by the perspective and bias of the historian attempting to give meaning to events.

This is why there is so much disagreement about the importance of some past events. You may have been taught in high school that it was important simply to learn dates and facts: that the Declaration of Independence was adopted on July 4, 1776, or that Franklin Roosevelt was inaugurated on March 4, 1933. But these facts by themselves are limited in meaning. They gain significance when they become parts of larger stories, such as why the American colonies revolted against England, or how America responded to the Great Depression. When historians construct stories or narratives in which these facts or events take on special significance, room for disagreement creeps in.

Since it is valid for historians to disagree, you should not automatically accept what any one historian writes. You should learn to apply general rules of logic and evidence in assessing the validity of different historical interpretations. This *Study Guide* will at times give you an opportunity to assess different interpretations of events. By doing this, you will learn to question what you read and hear, to think critically.

HOW TO READ A TEXTBOOK

Reading a textbook should be both pleasurable and profitable. The responsibility for this is partly the author's and partly yours, the reader's. George Tindall, David Shi, and Thomas Lee Pearcy have written a text that should teach and entertain. In order to get the most out of it, you must read actively and critically. One way to avoid passive, mindless reading is to write, underline, or highlight material by hand. Simply by highlighting or underlining pertinent passages in the textbook, you will later be better able to recall what you have read, and you will be able to review important material quickly. The key to effective highlighting is to be judicious about what you choose to mark. You should highlight key words and phrases, not whole sentences unless all the words are important. For example, the two paragraphs below show the way we would highlight them:

During the second half of the nineteenth century, an **a growing stream of migrants** flowed into the largely Indian and Hispanic West. Newspaper editors described western migration as a "flood tide." Millions of Anglo-Americans, African Americans, Mexicans, and European and Chinese immigrants transformed the patterns of western society and culture. **Most of the settlers were relatively prosperous white, native-born farming families.** Because of the expense of transportation, land, and supplies, the very poor could not afford to relocate. **Three-quarters of the western migrants were men.**

The largest number of foreign immigrants who settled in the West came from **northern Europe and Canada.** In the northern plains, Germans, Scandinavians, and Irish were especially numerous. Not surprisingly, these foreign settlers tended to **cluster together according to ethnic and kinship ties.**

After the collapse of Radical Republican rule in the South, thousands of **blacks began migrating west** from Kentucky, Tennessee, Louisiana, Arkansas, Mississippi, and Texas. Some 6,000 southern blacks arrived in Kansas in 1879 alone, and as many as 20,000 may have come the following year. They came to be **known as Exodusters,** making their exodus out of the South in **search of a haven from racism and poverty.**

Probably no two persons would agree on exactly what words in the passage should be underlined, but you can readily see that we have emphasized only the major points concerning immigrants.

Highlighting like this can be helpful, but even more useful in increasing your retention of the material is to jot down brief notes about what you read. Taking notes makes it easier to commit important points to memory. This will help especially when you review for a test.

ACKNOWLEDGMENTS

I wish to thank George B. Tindall, David E. Shi, and Thomas Lee Pearcy for having written the excellent text around which I developed this *Study Guide*. My hope is that the text and the *Study Guide* will combine to promote in students a clear understanding of the history of the United States. I have a great debt to Steven Forman and John Durbin, my editors at W. W. Norton & Company, who have again used their considerable skill to fashion the final product.

C.W.E.

THE ESSENTIAL AMERICA

AMERICA

STUDY GUIDE

VOLUME II

17 ∞

RECONSTRUCTION: NORTH AND SOUTH

CHAPTER OBJECTIVES

After you complete the reading and study of this chapter, you should be able to

1. Assess the impact of the Civil War on both the South and the North and on the status of freed blacks.
2. Outline the circumstances that led to Radical Reconstruction.
3. Describe the nature and extent of Radical Reconstruction.
4. Explain the process that returned control of the South to the conservatives.
5. Evaluate the contributions and failures of the Grant administration.
6. Understand the outcome of the election of 1876, the effects of that election, and the special arrangements made to conclude it.
7. Evaluate the overall impact of Reconstruction.

CHAPTER OUTLINE

I. The war's aftermath
  A. The North
    1. Friendly to business
    2. National power centralized
      a. Morrill Tariff
      b. National Banking Act
      c. Transcontinental railroad
      d. Homestead Act
      e. Morrill Land Grant Act
  B. The South
    1. Property destroyed
    2. Worthless money and bonds
    3. Slaves freed
    4. Relationships transformed
  C. The freed slaves
    1. New status
      a. Legal rights
      b. Lack of property
    2. Freedmen's Bureau
      a. Help freedmen
      b. Limited powers

II. Battle over Reconstruction
  A. Lincoln's plan
    1. Provisions
    2. Implementation
  B. Congressional reaction
    1. Radical critics
    2. Wade-Davis Bill
    3. Lincoln's response
  C. Assassination of Lincoln
  D. Johnson's plan
    1. Johnson's background
      a. Tennessee
      b. Jacksonian
      c. Unionist
      d. Election

2. Ideas on Union
   a. Indestructible
   b. No Reconstruction
3. Similar to Lincoln's plan
E. Southern resistance
   1. Elects ex-Confederates
   2. "Black codes"
F. Congressional Radicals
   1. Joint Committee on Reconstruction
   2. Motivation
   3. Constitutional theory
G. Johnson vs. Congress
   1. Veto of Freedmen's Bureau extension
   2. Johnson attacks Radicals
   3. Veto of Civil Rights Act overridden
   4. The Fourteenth Amendment

III. Congressional Reconstruction
A. Elections of 1866
B. Legislation
   1. Military Reconstruction Act
   2. Command of the Army Act
   3. Tenure of Office Act
   4. Limits on Supreme Court review
C. Impeachment and trial of Johnson
   1. Mutual hostility
   2. Initial effort failed
   3. Violation of Tenure in Office Act
   4. Political purposes
   5. Trial
   6. Effects of trial
D. Republican rule in South
   1. Readmission of states
   2. Role of Union League

IV. The reconstructed South
A. The life of freedmen
   1. Military experience
   2. Independent organizations
   3. Farm workers
      a. Wage laborers
      b. Tenant farmers
B. Black political life
   1. Increasing participation
   2. Divisions among blacks
   3. Limited political role
C. White Republicans in South
   1. Carpetbaggers

2. Scalawags
D. The Radicals' record
E. White terror
   1. Ku Klux Klan
   2. Enforcement Acts
F. Conservative resurgence
   1. Weakened morale
   2. Mobilized white vote
   3. Decline of northern concern

V. The Grant years
A. The election of 1868
   1. Reasons for support of Grant
   2. The Grant ticket and platform
   3. Democratic programs and candidates
   4. Results
   5. The character of Grant's leadership
B. Proposal to pay the government debt
C. Scandals
   1. Jay Gould's effort to corner the gold market
   2. The Crédit-Mobilier exposure
   3. Secretary of War and the Indian Bureau
   4. "Whiskey Ring"
   5. Grant's personal role in the scandals
D. Reform and the election of 1872
   1. Liberal Republicans nominate Greeley in 1872
   2. Grant's advantages
E. Economic panic
   1. Causes for the depression
   2. Severity of the depression
   3. Democratic control of the House in 1874
   4. Reissue of greenbacks
   5. Resumption of specie payments approved in 1875

VI. The Compromise of 1877
A. Election of 1876
   1. Republicans nominate Hayes
   2. Democrats run Tilden
   3. Uncertain results
B. Electoral Commission
C. Compromises
D. End of Reconstruction

KEY ITEMS OF CHRONOLOGY

Lincoln's plan for Reconstruction announced	1863
Thirteenth Amendment ratified	1865
Creation of Freedmen's Bureau	1865
Assassination of Lincoln	April 14, 1865
Johnson's plan for Reconstruction announced	May 29, 1865
Veto of Freedmen's Bureau Extension Bill	February 1866
Congress overrode Johnson's veto of Civil Rights Act	April 1866
Ku Klux Klan organized in the South	1866
Military Reconstruction Act	March 2, 1867
Johnson replaces Stanton with Grant as secretary of war	August 1867
House votes to impeach Johnson	February 1868
Trial of Johnson in Senate	March 5 to May 26, 1868
Fourteenth Amendment ratified	1868
All southern states except Mississippi, Texas, and Virginia, readmitted to Congress	June 1868
Texas v. *White* decision of Supreme Court	1868
Grant administrations	1869–1877
Mississippi, Texas, and Virginia readmitted	1870
Fifteenth Amendment ratified	1870
Resumption Act	1875

TERMS TO MASTER

Listed below are some important terms or people with which you should be familiar after you complete the study of this chapter. Explain or identify each.

1. Freedmen's Bureau
2. Wade-Davis Hill
3. Andrew Johnson
4. "iron clad" oath
5. black codes
6. Radicals
7. Joint Committee on Reconstruction
8. forfeited rights theory
9. Fourteenth Amendment
10. Military Reconstruction
11. Command of the Army Act
12. Tenure of Office Act
13. Edwin M. Stanton
14. sharecropper
15. black Reconstruction
16. carpetbaggers and scalawags
17. Ku Klux Klan
18. Liberal Republicans
19. hard money
20. Black Friday
21. Jay Gould
22. Crédit-Mobilier
23. Whiskey Ring
24. Horace Greeley
25. Panic of 1873
26. Rutherford B. Hayes
27. Samuel J. Tilden
28. Compromise of 1877

VOCABULARY BUILDING

Listed below are some words used in this chapter. Look in the dictionary for the meaning of each.

1. imposing
2. elite
3. disarray
4. haggle
5. assumption

6. platitudes
7. thwart
8. caste
9. collaborator
10. limbo
11. proprietor
12. provisional
13. vagrant
14. guise
15. fanatical
16. petulant
17. abridge
18. pragmatism
19. incubus
20. renegade
21. brethren
22. dissension
23. revile
24. crass
25. recalcitrant
26. mollify
27. odious
28. bilk
29. sterling
30. impasse

EXERCISES FOR UNDERSTANDING

When you have completed reading the chapter, answer each of the following questions. If you have difficulty, go back to the text and reread the section of the chapter related to the question.

Multiple-Choice Questions

Select the letter of the response that best completes the statement.

1. As a result of the Civil War, southerners lost investments worth $4 billion in
   A. cotton.
   B. railroads.
   C. slaves.
   D. tobacco.
2. The Freedmen's Bureau
   A. provided temporary relief and assistance to freedmen.
   B. effectively protected the economic rights of former slaves.
   C. turned over hundreds and thousands of acres of confiscated confederate lands to the freedmen.
   D. established schools and hospitals for the former slaves.
3. The Radical Republicans wanted
   A. Congress to direct Reconstruction.
   B. to transform southern society.
   C. to make the freed slaves full citizens.
   D. all of the above
4. Before becoming president, Andrew Johnson had been
   A. a Democrat.
   B. an abolitionist.
   C. a senator from Maine.
   D. all of the above
5. Andrew Johnson hated
   A. slavery.
   B. southern planters.
   C. Abraham Lincoln.
   D. all of the above
6. The term "black codes" refers to
   A. legislation passed by southern legislatures dominated by freedmen.
   B. the policies of Radical Republicans.
   C. southern laws restricting the freedom of blacks.
   D. the failed Reconstruction policies of Lincoln.
7. The phrases "due process of law" and "equal protection of the laws" are found in the
   A. Civil Rights Act of 1866.
   B. Thirteenth Amendment.
   C. Fourteenth Amendment.
   D. Fifteenth Amendment.
8. When it enacted the Tenure of Office Act, Congress had in mind
   A. Edwin Stanton.
   B. Thaddeus Stevens.
   C. Horace Greeley.
   D. Andrew Johnson.
9. The Radical southern governments during Reconstruction
   A. were unusually honest and moral.
   B. operated frugally and did not go into debt.
   C. refused to aid private corporations such as railroads.

D. gave unusual attention to education and poor relief.

10. As a result of his impeachment, President Johnson
    A. was removed from office.
    B. gained the upper hand in his fight with Congress over Reconstruction.
    C. lost considerable power and influence.
    D. decided to leave politics.

11. After the Civil War, most freed slaves became
    A. independent farmers.
    B. sharecroppers.
    C. industrial workers.
    D. skilled craftsmen and artisans.

12. Under Radical Reconstruction, black voters
    A. sent more than a dozen blacks to the U.S. Senate.
    B. elected three African Americans state governors.
    C. dominated the state legislatures.
    D. chose fourteen black congressmen.

13. A terrorist group started in 1866 in Pulaski, Tennessee, was the
    A. Union League.
    B. Ku Klux Klan.
    C. Greenbackers.
    D. Whiskey Ring.

14. In 1869, the gold market was almost cornered by
    A. Horace Greeley.
    B. Thaddeus Stevens and Charles Sumner.
    C. Jay Gould and Jim Fisk.
    D. James G. Blaine and P. B. S. Pinchback.

15. As a result of the Compromise of 1877,
    A. Rutherford Hayes became president.
    B. federal troops were withdrawn from Louisiana and South Carolina.
    C. southerners accepted the Fourteenth Amendment.
    D. all of the above

True-False Questions

Indicate whether each statement is true or false.

1. After the Civil War, each former slave received forty acres and a mule.

2. Lincoln claimed the right to direct Reconstruction under the presidential pardon power.

3. In 1864, Lincoln signed the Wade-Davis Bill for Reconstruction.

4. Andrew Johnson was a strong supporter of the Union.

5. Andrew Johnson's plan to restore the Union closely resembled Lincoln's.

6. Thaddeus Stevens and Charles Sumner were Radical Republicans.

7. In 1866, Andrew Johnson clashed with Congress over the Freedmen's Bureau.

8. As a result of the 1866 elections, President Johnson gained support in the Congress.

9. The impeachment of President Johnson was precipitated largely by his violation of the Tenure of Office Act.

10. After the conviction of President Johnson, the Radicals controlled Reconstruction.

11. Postwar southern black political leaders rarely had any military experience.

12. A scalawag was a northern white Republican who moved to the South.

13. U. S. Grant was elected president in 1868.

14. The Panic of 1873 was a mild economic setback that affected only the South.

15. Reconstruction came to an end in 1877.

Essay Questions

1. Did the Civil War have a greater impact on the North or on the South? Explain.

2. How did the Reconstruction plans of Lincoln, Johnson, and the Radicals differ? Which was the best? Why?

3. How did the southern states eventually return to control by southern whites?

4. Why was Andrew Johnson impeached? What was the outcome?

5. What were the major provisions of the Fourteenth Amendment?

6. Was Grant a successful president? Why or why not?

7. Explain the provisions of the Compromise of 1877 and its effects on the South.

ANSWERS TO MULTIPLE-CHOICE AND TRUE-FALSE QUESTIONS

Multiple-Choice Questions

1-C, 2-A, 3-D, 4-A, 5-B, 6-C, 7-C, 8-A, 9-D, 10-C, 11-B, 12-D, 13-B, 14-C, 15-D

True-False Questions

1-F, 2-T, 3-F, 4-T, 5-T, 6-T, 7-T, 8-F, 9-T, 10-F, 11-F, 12-F, 13-T, 14-F, 15-T

18 ∞

NEW FRONTIERS: SOUTH AND WEST

CHAPTER OBJECTIVES

After you complete the reading and study of this chapter, you should be able to

1. Analyze the concept of the New South, its development, and how it affected the South after the Civil War.
2. Account for the rise of the Bourbons to power in the South and explain their impact on the region.
3. Explain the causes and process of disenfranchisement of blacks in the South.
4. Compare the views of Washington and Du Bois on the place of blacks in American life.
5. Understand the process of settling the West.
6. Describe the Indian wars and explain the new Indian policy of 1887.
7. Assess the importance of violence in the culture of the West.
8. Appraise the problems of farming and ranching on the western frontier.
9. Explain the importance of Turner's theory of the significance of the frontier in American history.

CHAPTER OUTLINE

I. The New South
  A. Concept of the New South
    1. Henry Grady's vision
    2. The New South creed
  B. Economic growth
    1. Growth of cotton textile manufacturing
    2. Development of the tobacco industry
      a. Duke family
      b. The American Tobacco Company
    3. Coal production
    4. Lumbering
    5. Beginnings of petroleum and hydroelectric power
  C. Agriculture in the New South
    1. King Cotton
    2. Features of sharecropping and tenancy
    3. Impact of the crop lien system
  D. Role of the Bourbon Redeemers
    1. Nature of the Bourbons
    2. Bourbon economic policies
      a. Laissez-faire
      b. Retrenchment in government

     c. Private philanthropy
     d. Convict lease system
     e. Repudiation of Confederate debts in some states
     f. Positive contributions
     g. Varied development of color lines in social relations
   E. Disenfranchisement of blacks
    1. Impetus for elimination of the black vote
     a. Fears of retrogression
     b. Impact of Populists
    2. Techniques used to exclude blacks
     a. Mississippi
     b. Louisiana
   F. Spread of segregation
    1. Segregation in railway cars
    2. *Civil Rights Cases,* 1883
    3. *Plessy* v. *Ferguson,* 1896
   G. Spread of violence against blacks
   H. Clash of Booker T. Washington and W.E.B. Du Bois

II. The New West
   A. The West after the war
    1. Manifest Destiny or colonization
    2. Moving frontiers
    3. Changes in the Great American Desert
   B. Migration
    1. Sources
    2. African Americans
     a. Exodusters
     b. Cowboys and soldiers
   C. The mining frontier
    1. Pattern of mining development

    2. Locations of major mineral discoveries
    3. New states
   D. Indians
    1. Indian wars
     a. 1851 treaty with Plains tribes
     b. Wars in 1860s and 1870s
      i. Slaughter at Fort Lyon
      ii. Indian Peace Commission
       (a) Reservations
       (b) White encroachment
      iii. Red River War
      iv. The Great Sioux War
       (a) General George Custer
       (b) Little Bighorn
      v. Nez Percés
      vi. Wounded Knee
    2. Indian policy reform
     a. Concerns of easterners
     b. Dawes Severalty Act
   E. Cowboys and cattle on the range
    1. Cattle industry
     a. Mexican influence
     b. Railroads and cowtowns
     c. Cowboys
     d. Meat packers
     e. Barbed wire
    2. Range wars
   F. Farming
    1. Availability of land
    2. Hardships of farm life
    3. Pioneer women
   G. Violent culture
   H. Turner's frontier thesis
    1. Effects of frontier
    2. End of the frontier

KEY ITEMS OF CHRONOLOGY

Homestead Act	1862
First of the long drives	1866
Indian Peace Commission settlements	1867–1868
Civil Rights Cases	1883
Dawes Severalty Act	1887
Mississippi Constitution incorporates disenfranchisement of blacks	1890

Census shows frontier closed	1890
Turner frontier thesis presented	1893
B. T. Washington's "Atlanta Compromise" speech	1895
Plessy v. *Ferguson*	1896
Spideltop oil gusher	1901
Newlands Reclamation Act	1901
Disenfranchisement of blacks essentially completed in southern states	1910

TERMS TO MASTER

Listed below are some important terms or people with which you should be familiar after you complete the study of this chapter. Identify or explain each.

1. Henry W. Grady
2. American Tobacco Company
3. sharecropping
4. crop lien system
5. Bourbons
6. convict lease system
7. Mississippi Plan for disfranchisement
8. grandfather clause
9. Jim Crow
10. *Plessy* v. *Ferguson*
11. Booker T. Washington
12. W. E. B. Du Bois
13. Great American Desert
14. Exodusters
15. Buffalo Soldiers
16. George A. Custer
17. Great Sioux War
18. Geronimo
19. Wounded Knee
20. Dawes Severalty Act
21. Joseph Glidden
22. Newlands Reclamation Act
23. Sodbuster
24. Frederick Jackson Turner

VOCABULARY BUILDING

Listed below are some words used in this chapter. Look in the dictionary for the meaning of each.

1. enticing
2. wistfully
3. nostalgia
4. permeate
5. textile
6. impel
7. bonanza
8. prevalent
9. rhetoric
10. privation
11. austerity
12. scrimp
13. mongrel
14. paragon
15. gerrymander
16. petty
17. rubric
18. antagonize
19. dubious
20. inexorable
21. decimate
22. arid
23. vigilante
24. polygamy
25. encroach
26. decry
27. drudgery
28. spawn
29. unfettered
30. homogenize

EXERCISES FOR UNDERSTANDING

When you have completed reading the chapter, answer each of the following questions. If you have difficulty, go back and reread the section of the chapter related to the question.

Multiple-Choice Questions

Select the letter of the response that best completes the statement.

1. Henry Grady is best known for his support of
   A. disenfranchisement of blacks.
   B. diverse industry in the South.
   C. W. E. B. Du Bois.
   D. the Old South's plantation life.
2. The New South movement's major accomplishment was the expansion of the
   A. tobacco industry.
   B. power of state governments.
   C. textile industry.
   D. South's rail system.
3. The "Pittsburgh of the South" was
   A. Richmond.
   B. Atlanta.
   C. Nashville.
   D. Birmingham.
4. Bourbon policies included
   A. the convict lease system.
   B. repudiation of state debts.
   C. alliances with northeastern conservatives.
   D. all of the above
5. Mississippi disenfranchised blacks by means of
   A. residence requirements and a grandfather clause.
   B. literacy tests and a poll tax.
   C. understanding and grandfather clauses.
   D. a grandfather clause only.
6. In *Plessy* v. *Ferguson,* the Supreme Court approved
   A. disenfranchisement.
   B. poll taxes.
   C. state regulation of railroads.
   D. racial segregation.

7. The "Atlanta Compromise" speech was given by
   A. Henry Grady.
   B. W. E. B. Du Bois.
   C. Booker T. Washington.
   D. Homer Plessy.
8. In the late nineteenth century, most of the settlers in the West were
   A. immigrants from eastern Europe.
   B. prosperous, native-born, white farmers.
   C. immigrants from Asia and Mexico.
   D. white and black southerners.
9. In the Battle of Little Bighorn, Colonel George A. Custer fought
   A. gold and silver miners in Colorado.
   B. Indians in the Montana territory.
   C. "Calamity Jane" and "Wild Bill" Hickok in South Dakota.
   D. Indians in the Southwest.
10. The Dawes Severalty Act of 1887 dealt with
    A. the transcontinental railroads.
    B. ranchers and rights on the open range.
    C. the sales of homesteads in the West.
    D. Indian policy.
11. Refrigeration was the key to the growth of
    A. the cattle industry.
    B. urban centers in the West.
    C. travel by transcontinental railroad.
    D. the tobacco industry.
12. Western range wars pitted
    A. the army against Mexican invaders.
    B. Indians against miners.
    C. ranchers against farmers.
    D. railroads against buffaloes.
13. The Newlands Reclamation Act of 1901
    A. spurred irrigation.
    B. took western land from the Indians.
    C. acquired the final territory between the Atlantic and Pacific oceans.
    D. gave reservations to Indians.
14. The western frontier had disappeared, according to the superintendent of the census, by
    A. 1865.
    B. 1880.
    C. 1890.
    D. 1900.

15. The frontier thesis about American development was presented by
    A. Francis G. Newlands.
    B. Joseph Glidden.
    C. Joseph G. McCoy.
    D. Frederick Jackson Turner.

True-False Questions

Indicate whether each statement is true or false.

1. The Duke family created the American Tobacco Company.
2. Southern farmers suffered from inflation in the late 1800s.
3. Sharecroppers supplied everything but the land to be farmed.
4. In the postwar South, Bourbons lost political power to the Redeemers.
5. Southern states used primaries to prevent blacks from voting.
6. Jim Crow involved racial segregation.
7. Booker T. Washington earned a Ph.D. from Harvard University.
8. Exodusters were southern blacks migrating to the West.
9. Blacks failed in their attempts to become cowboys.
10. Democrats opposed admitting new western states because they were Republican strongholds.
11. Geronimo was captured at the Battle of Wounded Knee in 1886.
12. Joseph Glidden invented barbed wire.
13. The lack of water shaped western institutions more than land laws did.
14. Most settlers in the West obtained their lands directly from the government.
15. The West in 1890 contained equal numbers of men and women.

Essay Questions

1. What was the New South and how did it really differ from the Old South?
2. How did race relations in the South change in the late nineteenth century?
3. What were the major differences between Booker T. Washington and W. E. B. Du Bois? Which had the greater impact around 1900 and later in the twentieth century?
4. What factors influenced the settlement and development of the West in the late 1800s?
5. How did public attitudes and governmental policies toward Indians resemble those toward blacks?
6. By 1900, was the South or the West more developed and prosperous? Why?

ANSWERS TO MULTIPLE-CHOICE AND TRUE-FALSE QUESTIONS

Multiple-Choice Questions

1-B, 2-C, 3-D, 4-D, 5-B, 6-D, 7-C, 8-B, 9-B, 10-D, 11-A, 12-C, 13-A, 14-C, 15-D

True-False Questions

1-T, 2-F, 3-F, 4-F, 5-T, 6-T, 7-F, 8-T, 9-F, 10-T, 11-F, 12-T, 13-T, 14-F, 15-F

19 ⚭

BIG BUSINESS AND ORGANIZED LABOR

CHAPTER OBJECTIVES

After you complete the reading and study of this chapter, you should be able to

1. Evaluate the economic impact of the Civil War.
2. Understand the important factors in the growth of the economy in the late nineteenth century.
3. Discuss the role of the major entrepreneurs like Rockefeller, Carnegie, and Morgan.
4. Account for the limited growth of unions in this period and the success of the Knights of Labor and the American Federation of Labor.
5. Describe the major labor confrontations in this period.
6. Explain the limited appeal of socialism for American labor.

CHAPTER OUTLINE

I. The rise of big business
   A. Second industrial revolution
      1. Interconnected national networks
         a. Transportation
         b. Communications
      2. Electric power

3. Scientific research
   B. Railroads
      1. First big business
      2. Transcontinental railroad
         a. Pacific Railway Act
            i. Union Pacific
            ii. Central Pacific
         b. Chinese labor
         c. Promontory, Utah
      3. Financing railroads
         a. Private companies
         b. Government aid
         c. Robber barons
   C. Manufacturing and inventions
      1. Patents
      2. Alexander Graham Bell
      3. Thomas Edison

II. Entrepreneurs
   A. John D. Rockefeller
      1. Background
      2. Standard Oil
      3. Vertical integration
      4. Trust
      5. Holding company
      6. Philanthropist
   B. Andrew Carnegie
      1. Background
      2. Iron and bridges
      3. Innovations in steel

4. "The Gospel of Wealth"
C. J. Pierpont Morgan
  1. Background
  2. Investment banker
  3. Railroads
  4. U.S. Steel Corporation
D. Sears and Roebuck
  1. Retailing
  2. Sears, Roebuck and Company
  3. Sears catalog

III. Labor conditions and organizations
A. Circumstances for workers
  1. Wages and hours
  2. Living and working conditions
B. Obstacles to unions
C. Molly Maguires
D. Railroad strike of 1877
  1. Causes
  2. Scope and violence
  3. Effects
  4. Impact on California
E. Efforts at union building
  1. National Labor Union
  2. Knights of Labor
    a. Early development
    b. Emphasis on the union
    c. Role of Terence Powderly

d. Victories of the Knights
e. Anarchism
f. Haymarket Affair
g. Lasting influence of the Knights of Labor
3. Development of the American Federation of Labor
  a. Development of craft unions
  b. Role of Samuel Gompers
  c. Growth of the union
F. Violence in the 1890s
  1. Homestead Strike, 1892
  2. Pullman Strike, 1894
    a. Causes
    b. Role of the government
    c. Impact on Eugene V. Debs
G. Socialism and American labor
  1. Daniel DeLeon and Eugene Debs
  2. Social Democratic party
    a. Early work
    b. Height of influence
  3. Rise of the IWW
    a. Sources of strength
    b. Revolutionary goals
    c. Causes for decline
IV. Effects of industrial revolution

KEY ITEMS OF CHRONOLOGY

National Labor Union formed	1866
Completion of the first transcontinental railroad	1869
Knights of Labor started	1869
Standard Oil of Ohio incorporated	1870
Telephone patented	1876
Great Railroad Strike	1877
Incandescent light bulb invented	1879
Terence Powderly became president of the Knights of Labor	1879
First electric current supplied to eighty-five customers in New York City	1882
Congress barred Chinese immigrants	1882
Creation of the Standard Oil Trust	1882
Haymarket Affair	1886
Founding of the American Federation of Labor	1886
Homestead Strike	1892

Pullman Strike	1894
U.S. Steel Corporation formed	1901
IWW founded	1905
IWW textile strike in Lawrence, Mass.	1912

TERMS TO MASTER

Listed below are some important terms or people with which you should be familiar after you complete the study of this chapter. Identify or explain each.

1. second industrial revolution
2. Union Pacific
3. transcontinental railroads
4. Cornelius Vanderbilt
5. Alexander Graham Bell
6. Thomas Alva Edison
7. George Westinghouse
8. "Battle of the Currents"
9. John D. Rockefeller
10. Standard Oil Company of Ohio
11. vertical integration
12. trust (n.)
13. holding company
14. Andrew Carnegie
15. Bessemer process
16. Gospel of Wealth
17. J. Pierpont Morgan
18. United States Steel Corporation
19. Richard Sears
20. Molly Maguires
21. Great Railroad Strike of 1877
22. Dennis Kearney
23. industrial and craft unions
24. National Labor Union
25. Knights of Labor
26. Terence V. Powderly
27. Haymarket Affair
28. American Federation of Labor
29. Samuel Gompers
30. Homestead Strike
31. Pullman Strike
32. Eugene V. Debs
33. Wobblies
34. William D. Haywood

VOCABULARY BUILDING

Listed below are some words used in this chapter. Look in the dictionary for the meaning of each.

1. cope
2. entrepreneur
3. dissent
4. exploit
5. scruple
6. revenue
7. consolidate
8. financier
9. guile
10. devout
11. clout
12. dissuade
13. philanthropist
14. scorn
15. dreary
16. agrarian
17. transient
18. impromptu
19. incite
20. quell
21. scapegoat
22. agitator
23. utopian
24. arbitration
25. reprieve
26. tedium
27. jurisdictional
28. wrack
29. manifesto
30. ardent

EXERCISES FOR UNDERSTANDING

When you have completed reading the chapter, answer each of the following questions. If you have difficulty, go back and reread the section of the chapter related to the question.

Multiple-Choice Questions

Select the letter of the response that best completes the statement.

1. The second industrial revolution involved
   A. creation of a national market.
   B. use of electric power.
   C. application of scientific research to industry.
   D. all of the above

2. Union Pacific work crews on the transcontinental railroad were primarily
   A. Native Americans.
   B. Chinese.
   C. former slaves.
   D. members of the Knights of Labor.

3. Cornelius Vanderbilt's great achievement was in
   A. merchandising.
   B. education.
   C. railroads.
   D. electricity.

4. Ending dependence on other firms known as middlemen is called
   A. monopoly.
   B. trust.
   C. holding company.
   D. vertical integration.

5. John D. Rockefeller made his fortune in
   A. oil.
   B. banking.
   C. railroads.
   D. real estate.

6. Andrew Carnegie's *Gospel of Wealth* called on the rich to
   A. support overseas missionaries.
   B. get richer.
   C. provide for the public good.
   D. help others gain wealth by turning their businesses over to workers.

7. United States Steel Corporation was started by
   A. J. P. Morgan.
   B. John D. Rockefeller.
   C. Cornelius Vanderbilt.
   D. Jim Fisk and Jay Cooke.

8. Sears and Roebuck transformed
   A. clothing manufacturing.
   B. retailing.
   C. publishing, especially of catalogs.
   D. advertising.

9. J. P. Morgan made his wealth in
   A. investments.
   B. railroads.
   C. steel.
   D. all of the above

10. Between 1860 and 1890, real wages and earning in industry
    A. increased by 50 percent for workers.
    B. increased only for management and owners.
    C. declined by 25 percent due to inflation.
    D. stayed roughly the same for workers while the rich prospered.

11. The group trying to protect coal miners in eastern Pennsylvania during the 1870s was the
    A. Knights of Labor.
    B. Wobblies.
    C. Pinkertons led by Dennis Kearney.
    D. Molly Maguires.

12. The Knights of Labor
    A. led the Great Railroad Strike of 1877.
    B. limited its membership to skilled craftsmen.
    C. called for equal pay for equal work for men and women.
    D. all of the above

13. The Haymarket Affair of 1886 grew out of
    A. clashes between the Ku Klux Klan and the Wobblies in Pennsylvania.
    B. a strike at an International Harvester plant in Chicago.
    C. Carnegie's suppression of unions in his steel mills.
    D. Dennis Kearney's attempts to organize farm workers in California.

14. The most important walkout in American labor history occurred at
    A. Haymarket in 1886.
    B. Homestead in 1892.
    C. Pullman in 1894.
    D. Lawrence, Massachusetts, in 1912.
15. The Industrial Workers of the World was led by
    A. Samuel Gompers.
    B. William Haywood.
    C. Terence Powderly.
    D. Henry C. Frick.

10. Terence V. Powderly was the leader of the Molly Maguires.
11. The American Federation of Labor was a federation of craft unions.
12. The public associated the American Federation of Labor with anarchists.
13. The American Federation of Labor sought concrete economic gains rather than utopian reforms.
14. Henry C. Frick squashed the strikers at Pullman.
15. Eugene Debs ran for president as a candidate of the Socialist party.

True-False Questions

Indicate whether each statement is true or false.

1. The new national market led to mass production and distribution.
2. The first transcontinental railroad was completed in 1859.
3. Alexander Graham Bell patented the telephone.
4. In the "Battle of the Currents," Edison's direct current lost to Westinghouse's alternating current.
5. The world's leading philanthropist was J. P. Morgan.
6. John D. Rockefeller was born in Scotland.
7. Thomas Edison invented the phonograph.
8. Most industrial leaders in the late nineteenth century had started as inventors.
9. The first major interstate strike was the Great Railroad Strike of 1877.

Essay Questions

1. What factors promoted the growth of industry in the United States in the late nineteenth century?
2. Why were railroads crucial to the economic changes in the late nineteenth century?
3. What was the relationship among inventors, entrepreneurs, and great wealth in the late–nineteenth-century United States? Give several examples.
4. What were the major conflicts between labor and capitalists in the late nineteenth century? What effects did they have?
5. How did the goals and tactics of the Knights of Labor differ from those of the Wobblies? Which were more effective?
6. How did the economy of the United States change between the Civil War and 1900?

ANSWERS TO MULTIPLE-CHOICE AND TRUE-FALSE QUESTIONS

Multiple-Choice Questions

1-D, 2-B, 3-C, 4-D, 5-A, 6-C, 7-A, 8-B, 9-D, 10-A, 11-D, 12-C, 13-B, 14-C, 15-B

True-False Questions

1-T, 2-F, 3-T, 4-T, 5-F, 6-F, 7-T, 8-F, 9-T, 10-F, 11-T, 12-F, 13-T, 14-F, 15-T

20

THE EMERGENCE OF URBAN AMERICA

CHAPTER OBJECTIVES

After you complete the reading and study of this chapter, you should be able to

1. Understand the important intellectual trends in the period 1877–1890.
2. Describe city growth in the late nineteenth century.
3. Account for the new immigration and the reaction that it engendered.
4. Discuss the developments in urban popular culture in the late nineteenth century.
5. Trace major developments in higher education after the Civil War.
6. Understand the concepts of Social Darwinism and Reform Darwinism.
7. Discuss the local-color, realist, and naturalist movements in literature.
8. Explain the social gospel and describe its manifestations.

CHAPTER OUTLINE

I. Urbanization
  A. Location of urban growth
    1. Pacific coast
    2. The South

B. Types of growth
  1. Vertical
    a. Steam heat
    b. Elevator
    c. Steel frame
    d. Skyscraper
  2. Horizontal
    a. Mass transit
    b. Bridges
    c. Suburbs
C. Assets and liabilities of cities
  1. Urban attractions
  2. Urban problems
    a. Crowding
    b. Public health
    c. Mortality rate
D. Urban politics
  1. Political machines
  2. City services

II. New immigration
  A. America's attraction
  B. New immigrants from southern and eastern Europe
  C. Ellis Island
  D. Experience in America
    1. Exploitation
    2. Communities
      a. Ethnic
      b. Kinship

E. The nativist response
   1. Types of prejudice
   2. Immigration restriction
     a. Early attempts
     b. Chinese exclusion

III. Popular culture
  A. Distinctive urban culture
   1. Politics
   2. Mass entertainment
  B. Wild West shows
  C. Vaudeville
  D. Outdoor recreation
   1. Parks
   2. Tennis
   3. Bicycling
  E. Working-class recreation
   1. Street corners and sidewalks
   2. Saloons and dance halls
   3. Coney Island
  F. Spectator sports
   1. Urban locale
   2. Football
   3. Basketball
   4. Baseball

IV. Growth of education
  A. Public education
   1. Americanizing immigrants
   2. Increased enrollment
  B. Higher education
   1. Growth of colleges
   2. Elective system
   3. More opportunities for women
   4. Graduate education
  C. The rise of professionalism

V. Realist thought
  A. Rise of realism
   1. Different from idealism
   2. Contributing factors
     a. Civil War
     b. Modern science
  B. Darwinism and Social Darwinism
   1. *On the Origin of Species*

   2. Application to human society
     a. Social Darwinism
     b. Herbert Spencer
   3. Reform Darwinism
     a. Lester Frank Ward
     b. Role of government
  C. Pragmatism
   1. Ideas of William James
   2. Instrumentalism of John Dewey
  D. Literature
   1. Howells, Mark Twain, and James
   2. Literary Naturalism
     a. Frank Norris
     b. Stephen Crane
     c. Jack London
     d. Theodore Dreiser
  E. Social criticism
   1. Henry George and the single tax
   2. Henry Demarest Lloyd
   3. Veblen and conspicuous consumption

VI. The Social Gospel
  A. The church and the working class
   1. Neglect of inner city
   2. New organizations
     a. YMCA
     b. Salvation Army
  B. Washington Gladden
  C. Catholics' social doctrine

VII. Early efforts at urban reform
  A. Settlement house movement
   1. Jane Addams
   2. Activities
  B. Women's rights
   1. Gains in employment
   2. Suffrage movement
     a. Conflicts in movement
     b. Gains in the states
   3. Women's organizations
  C. Development of welfare policies
   1. Regulation of business and labor
   2. Urban machines

KEY ITEMS OF CHRONOLOGY

First football game	1869
Henry George's *Progress and Poverty*	1879

Publication of *Dynamic Sociology*	1883
Publication of *Huckleberry Finn*	1883
First electric elevator	1889
Basketball invented	1891
Electric streetcar systems in cities	1890s
Chinese Exclusion Act	1892
Ellis Island opened	1892
Publication of *Maggie: A Girl of the Streets*	1893
Veblen's *Theory of the Leisure Class*	1899

TERMS TO MASTER

Listed below are some important terms or people with which you should be familiar after you complete the study of this chapter. Identify or explain each.

1. streetcar suburbs
2. mass transit
3. "new" immigrants
4. Ellis Island
5. Chinese Exclusion Act
6. Angel Island
7. Buffalo Bill
8. vaudeville
9. James Naismith
10. Negro Leagues
11. elective system
12. professionalism
13. realism
14. Social Darwinism
15. Lester Frank Ward
16. pragmatism
17. William James
18. John Dewey
19. Henry James
20. naturalism
21. Theodore Dreiser
22. Henry George
23. Henry Demarest Lloyd
24. conspicuous consumption
25. Washington Gladden
26. social gospel
27. settlement houses
28. Susan B. Anthony
29. National American Woman Suffrage Association

VOCABULARY BUILDING

Listed below are some words used in this chapter. Look in the dictionary for the meaning of each.

1. ethnic
2. ramshackle
3. affluent
4. tenor
5. antebellum
6. cumbersome
7. noxious
8. graft (n.)
9. propaganda
10. influx
11. discretionary
12. bequeath
13. seedy
14. decorum
15. palatial
16. lambaste
17. mayhem
18. sedentary
19. guild
20. idealistic
21. empirical
22. shrewdness
23. pervasive
24. ameliorate
25. benevolent
26. expatriate
27. dogma
28. flaunt
29. prerogative
30. precursor

EXERCISES FOR UNDERSTANDING

When you have completed the reading of the chapter, answer each of the following questions. If you have difficulty, go back and reread the section of the chapter related to the question.

Multiple-Choice Questions

Select the letter of the response that best completes the statement.

1. At the turn of the century the most urban area of the United States was
   A. the Pacific coast.
   B. the South.
   C. New England.
   D. the Middle West.
2. Construction of buildings of more than three or four stories were made possible by
   A. bricks.
   B. steel frames.
   C. electric streetcars.
   D. steam heat.
3. The busiest year at Ellis Island was
   A. 1887.
   B. 1897.
   C. 1907.
   D. 1917.
4. In the 1890s, immigrants were refused entrance if they were
   A. illiterate.
   B. unemployed.
   C. Catholic or Jewish.
   D. criminals.
5. For recreation, the urban working class preferred
   A. vaudeville.
   B. cycling.
   C. viewing the stereopticon.
   D. saloons and dance halls.
6. Theodore Roosevelt intervened in football in 1905 because
   A. immigrants began to dominate the professional teams.
   B. his alma mater (Harvard) lost all its games.
   C. it had become too rough and dangerous.
   D. gambling had taken control of the game.

7. In 1891, Dr. Alexander Naismith invented
   A. football.
   B. basketball.
   C. baseball.
   D. rugby.
8. Advocates of public education wanted to
   A. Americanize immigrant children.
   B. prepare a skilled work force for industry.
   C. create patronage jobs for political machines.
   D. expand amateur athletics.
9. A new trend in higher education after the Civil War was
   A. the rise of graduate schools.
   B. coeducation.
   C. a return to a classical curriculum.
   D. all of the above
10. In literature, an emphasis on technology, factories, workers, and cities characterized
    A. idealism.
    B. realism.
    C. naturalism.
    D. modernism.
11. Social Darwinists advocated
    A. government regulation of railroads.
    B. building codes and housing regulation.
    C. laissez-faire policies.
    D. all of the above
12. In *Dynamic Sociology*, Lester Frank Ward argued that
    A. government should not interfere with social evolution.
    B. competition promoted human progress.
    C. Herbert Spencer's position made complete sense.
    D. humans could shape the process of evolution.
13. In the half-century after the Civil War, the American literary scene was dominated by
    A. Mark Twain.
    B. Henry James.
    C. Henry Demarest Lloyd.
    D. William Dean Howells.
14. The "theory of the leisure class" and "conspicuous consumption" were ideas of
    A. Henry George.
    B. Stephen Crane.
    C. Thorstein Veblen.
    D. Lester Frank Ward.

15. Before 1917, states adopting women's suffrage were in the
    A. East.
    B. West.
    C. South.
    D. industrial Northeast.

True-False Questions

Indicate whether each statement is true or false.

1. As people began to segregate along economic class lines with the emergence of suburbs, the wealthy dominated the central cities.
2. Urban political machines developed to provide needed city services.
3. After 1890, most immigrants came from southern and eastern Europe.
4. In 1882, Congress passed a law suspending Chinese immigration.
5. William Cody was a popular entertainer in the late nineteenth century.
6. Vaudeville houses appealed only to the upper classes.
7. Football was the most democratic sport in the nation.
8. Professional baseball was segregated in the early twentieth century.
9. The first major prophet of Social Darwinism was Lester Frank Ward.
10. Both William James and John Dewey were Social Darwinists.
11. Henry James, the novelist, was the brother of William James, the philosopher.
12. *The Red Badge of Courage* is an example of naturalistic writing.
13. Henry George advocated the single tax.
14. Susan B. Anthony started Hull House in Chicago.
15. In 1900 the most common form of employment for women was domestic work.

Essay Questions

1. In what ways was the American city of 1900 different from its counterpart in 1800?
2. How did urbanization spawn reform movements?
3. What changes occurred in American education in the decades after the Civil War?
4. How were Charles Darwin's ideas applied to understanding human societies?
5. What were the differences among idealism, realism, and naturalism in literature?
6. How did American women respond to the emergence of urban America?

ANSWERS TO MULTIPLE-CHOICE AND TRUE-FALSE QUESTIONS

Multiple-Choice Questions

1-A, 2-B, 3-C, 4-D, 5-D, 6-C, 7-B, 8-A, 9-A, 10-B, 11-C, 12-D, 13-D, 14-C, 15-B

True-False Questions

1-F, 2-T, 3-T, 4-T, 5-T, 6-F, 7-F, 8-T, 9-F, 10-F, 11-T, 12-T, 13-T, 14-F, 15-T

21

GILDED-AGE POLITICS
AND AGRARIAN REVOLT

CHAPTER OBJECTIVES

After you complete the reading and study of this chapter, you should be able to

1. Describe the major features of politics in the late nineteenth century.
2. Delineate the political alignments and issues in the "third political system."
3. Identify the major issues in the presidential elections of 1888, 1892, and 1896.
4. Account for the rise of the farmers' protest movement of the 1890s.
5. Explain the impact of populism on the American scene.

CHAPTER OUTLINE

I. Nature of Gilded-Age politics
  A. Paradoxical characteristics
    1. Stalemate but high participation
    2. "Real" and crucial issues
  B. Partisan politics
    1. Reasons for loyalty
      a. Patronage
      b. Entertainment
      c. Religious and ethnic bases
    2. Republican party
    3. Democratic party

  4. Religious and social issues
  C. National stalemate
    1. Even division between parties
    2. Deferential presidents
    3. Divided Congress
  D. State and local politics
    1. Active governments
    2. Regulation of corporations
    3. Judicial responses
      a. Initial support
      b. Opposition to state efforts
      c. Use of Fourteenth Amendment
II. Politics, corruption, and reform
  A. Attitudes toward corruption
    1. General tolerance
    2. Ties between business and politics
    3. "Spoils" of office
  B. Hayes and civil service reform
    1. Hayes's background
    2. Divisions among Republicans
    3. Support for reform
    4. Hayes's limited view
  C. James Garfield and Chester Arthur
    1. Election of 1880
      a. Nominees
      b. Results
    2. Garfield's assassination
    3. Arthur as president

      a. Support for civil service
      b. Support for tariff reform
  D. Election of 1884
    1. Republican James G. Blaine
      a. Background
      b. Allegations of corruption
      c. Mugwumps
    2. Democrat Grover Cleveland
      a. Background
      b. Illegitimate child
      c. "Rum, Romanism, and rebellion"
    3. Results
  E. Cleveland's presidency
    1. Cleveland's idea of government
    2. Stances on issues
      a. Civil service reform
      b. Union veterans
      c. Railroad regulation
      d. Tariff reform
  F. Election of 1888
    1. Nominations
    2. Republican victory
  G. Harrison administration
    1. Veterans' benefits
    2. Republican Congress
      a. Sherman Antitrust Act
      b. Sherman Silver Purchase Act
      c. McKinley Tariff
    3. 1890 Democratic election victory

III. Farmers: their problems and protests
  A. Obstacles to collective action
    1. Individualism
    2. Isolation
    3. Pride
    4. Diversity
  B. Worsening conditions
    1. Declining commodity prices
    2. Railroads as villains

    3. Disadvantageous tariff
    4. Burdensome debt
  C. Granger movement
    1. Origins
    2. Political activity
  D. Farmers' Alliances
    1. Background
    2. Membership
    3. Appeal of Alliances
    4. Political activity
      a. Cooperatives
      b. Subtreasury
      c. Third party
      d. Mary Lease
  E. Populist party in 1892 election
    1. Platform
    2. Nominees
    3. Results

IV. The economy, silver, and politics
  A. The currency and money supply
    1. Deflation
    2. Metallic currency
    3. "Crime of 1873"
  B. Depression of 1893
    1. Wall Street panic
    2. Unemployment and strikes
    3. Bank failures
    4. "Coxey's Army"
    5. Republican victory in 1894
  C. Currency issue
    1. Repeal of Sherman Silver Purchase Act
    2. Demands for silver coinage
  D. Election of 1896
    1. McKinley and gold
    2. Bryan and silver
    3. Role of Populists
    4. Results
    5. A New Era

KEY ITEMS OF CHRONOLOGY

Patrons of Husbandry founded	1867
Hayes administration	1877–1881
Munn v. *Illinois*	1877
Bland-Allison Act	1878
Garfield administration	March–September 1881

Arthur administration	September 1881–1885
Pendleton Civil Service Act	1883
Mongrel Tariff Act	1883
Cleveland administrations	1885–1889; 1893–1897
Wabash v. *Illinois*	1886
Interstate Commerce Act	1887
Harrison administration	1889–1893
Sherman Anti-Trust Act	1890
Sherman Silver Purchase Act	1890
McKinley Tariff Act	1890
Populist party founded	1892
Economic depression	1893
McKinley administrations	1897–1901

TERMS TO MASTER

Listed below are some important terms or people with which you should be familiar after you complete the study of this chapter. Identify or explain each.

1. Gilded Age
2. *Munn* v. *Illinois*
3. *Wabash* v. *Illinois*
4. Fourteenth Amendment
5. spoils of office
6. civil service reform
7. Stalwarts and Half-Breeds
8. James G. Blaine
9. Pendleton Civil Service Act
10. Mongrel Tariff (1883)
11. Grover Cleveland
12. Mugwumps
13. Sherman Antitrust Act
14. Sherman Silver Purchase Act
15. McKinley Tariff
16. Patrons of Husbandry
17. Farmers' Alliances
18. subtreasury system
19. Mary Elizabeth Lease
20. Populist party
21. 16:1
22. depression of 1893
23. Coxey's Army
24. goldbug
25. William Jennings Bryan
26. William McKinley

VOCABULARY BUILDING

Listed below are some words used in this chapter. Look in the dictionary for the meaning of each.

1. vulgarity
2. inertia
3. stalemate
4. precarious
5. disenfranchisement
6. paradox
7. carouse
8. heterogeneous
9. nativist
10. patronage
11. thwart
12. faction
13. snide
14. eke
15. deranged
16. scurrilous
17. consummate
18. baron
19. charisma
20. candor
21. fiasco
22. bolster
23. linger
24. constituent
25. cohesive
26. lien
27. stigma
28. fluctuation
29. fiscal
30. fervent

EXERCISES FOR UNDERSTANDING

When you have completed reading the chapter, answer each of the following questions. If you have difficulty, go back and reread the section of the chapter related to the question.

Multiple-Choice Questions

Select the letter of the response that best completes the statement.

1. Politics in the Gilded Age was characterized by
   A. low voter turnout in elections.
   B. evenly balanced parties in all areas of the nation.
   C. low expectations of the federal government.
   D. weak local governments.
2. In the late nineteenth century, the party of Protestant moralists, antiCatholic nativists, and people of Yankee stock was the
   A. Democratic party.
   B. Republican party.
   C. Populist party.
   D. none of the above—there were no such distinctions among the parties.
3. The only major national issue that consistently divided the Democrats and Republicans was
   A. prohibition.
   B. regulation of business.
   C. civil service reform.
   D. tariff policy.
4. In *Munn* v. *Illinois,* the Supreme Court
   A. ruled state minimum wage laws were unconstitutional.
   B. said states could regulate industries vital to the public welfare.
   C. decided the spoils system for filling offices was unconstitutional.
   D. upheld the Sherman Antitrust Act.
5. James A. Garfield was
   A. the only president reelected between 1872 and 1896.
   B. assassinated while in office.
   C. defeated for reelection because of scandals in his administration.

D. impeached and removed from office in 1881.
6. "Ma, ma, where's my pa? Gone to the White House, ha, ha, ha!" was used against
   A. James A. Garfield.
   B. James G. Blaine.
   C. Winfield Scott.
   D. Grover Cleveland.
7. To regulate railroad rates, Congress passed the
   A. Sherman Antitrust Act.
   B. Pendleton Act.
   C. Mongrel Tariff.
   D. Interstate Commerce Act.
8. Cleveland challenged special interests most directly over
   A. civil service reform.
   B. tariff rates.
   C. regulation of railroads.
   D. prohibition.
9. The Sherman Silver Purchase Act of 1890
   A. reduced the government's purchases of silver.
   B. led to the inflation desired by farmers.
   C. worried eastern business and financial groups.
   D. all of the above
10. Farmers had difficulty organizing because of
    A. physical isolation.
    B. individualism.
    C. different economic interests.
    D. all of the above
11. The basic problem of farmers in the late nineteenth century was
    A. high railroad rates.
    B. overproduction of agricultural products.
    C. inflation.
    D. high prices for manufactured goods caused by high tariffs.
12. The Grange's chief political goal was
    A. the break-up of trusts and monopolies.
    B. regulation banks and insurance companies.
    C. unlimited coinage of silver.
    D. regulation of railroads and warehouses.
13. Jacob S. Coxey and his "army" demanded
    A. pensions for Civil War veterans.
    B. unlimited coinage of silver.

C. relief for the unemployed.
D. war with Spain.
14. In 1896, the Democratic candidate for president was
    A. William McKinley.
    B. Grover Cleveland.
    C. Theodore Roosevelt.
    D. William Jennings Bryan.
15. In 1896, the Populist candidate for president was
    A. Jacob Coxey.
    B. James B. Weaver.
    C. William Macune.
    D. William Jennings Bryan.

True-False Questions

Indicate whether each statement is true or false.

1. Immigrants and Jews tended to support the Democratic party.
2. Between 1872 and 1896, no president won a majority of the popular vote.
3. In the late nineteenth century, for the first time, federal employees outnumbered state and local workers.
4. To overturn state attempts to regulate business, the Supreme Court relied on the Fifteenth Amendment.
5. Stalwarts and Half-Breeds split the Republican party.
6. Chester A. Arthur surprised many by supporting civil service reform.

7. "Rum, Romanism, and rebellion" referred to Democrats.
8. In 1888, Grover Cleveland got more popular votes than his opponents but lost the election.
9. The Sherman Antitrust Act was used in the 1890s to break up scores of monopolies.
10. The McKinley Tariff of 1890 lowered rates dramatically.
11. In the late 1800s, the debts of farmers increased.
12. The Grange tried to solve the farmers' problems through cooperatives for buying and selling.
13. The Farmers' Alliance advocated the subtreasury system.
14. The Populists supported an income tax.
15. The first important act of the McKinley administration was to lower the tariff.

Essay Questions

1. How did local and national issues differ in Gilded Age politics?
2. Who was the most successful president in the Gilded Age? Why?
3. What issues divided the political parties in the late nineteenth century?
4. How and why did the farmers' protest movements develop?
5. Why was silver such an important issue in the Gilded Age?
6. What was the significance of the election of 1896?

ANSWERS TO MULTIPLE-CHOICE AND TRUE-FALSE QUESTIONS

Multiple-Choice Questions

1-C, 2-B, 3-D, 4-B, 5-B, 6-D, 7-D, 8-B, 9-C, 10-D, 11-B, 12-D, 13-C, 14-D, 15-D

True-False Questions

1-T, 2-T, 3-F, 4-F, 5-T, 6-T, 7-T, 8-T, 9-F, 10-F, 11-T, 12-T, 13-T, 14-T, 15-F

22

AN AMERICAN EMPIRE

CHAPTER OBJECTIVES

After you complete the reading and study of this chapter, you should be able to

1. Explain why the United States pursued a policy of imperialism.
2. Account for the outbreak of the Spanish-American War.
3. Trace the course of United States relations with Latin America during the late nineteenth century and its impact on later relations with Latin America.
4. Contrast the arguments in 1899 for and against imperialism.
5. Explain the development of America's policy for dealing with its imperial possessions.
6. Discuss the acquisition of the Panama Canal.
7. Assess the foreign policies of Theodore Roosevelt and William Howard Taft.

CHAPTER OUTLINE

I. The new imperialism
  A. Global context
    1. Economic sources
    2. Europeans in Asia and Africa
  B. American imperialism
    1. Extra-continental territories
    2. Debate over expansion
    3. Alfred Thayer Mahan
  C. Imperialist theories
    1. Anglo-Saxon superiority
    2. Christian mission
  D. Initial expansion in the Pacific
    1. Seward's purchase of Alaska
    2. Samoa
    3. Hawaii
      a. Trade agreement
      b. American intervention
      c. Republic of Hawaii
      d. Annexation

II. Spanish-American War
  A. Trouble in Cuba
    1. Spanish rule
    2. American interests
    3. "Butcher" Weyler
    4. "Yellow journalism"
  B. Pressure for war
    1. McKinley and Cuban independence
    2. Public opinion aroused
      a. de Lôme letter
      b. Sinking of the *Maine*
  C. Movement to war
    1. "Remember the *Maine*"

2. Congressional action
   a. Defense appropriation
   b. Teller Amendment
   c. Declaration of war
3. Reasons for war

D. The war
  1. Dewey's Manila victory
  2. Cuban campaign
   a. Rough Riders
   b. Attack on San Juan Hill
   c. Battle of Santiago
  3. Armistice

E. Debate over annexation
  1. Treaty of Paris
  2. Proponents of annexation
  3. Anti-imperialists
  4. Ratification of treaty
  5. Filipino guerrilla war

F. Organizing the acquisitions
  1. Philippines under Taft
  2. Government for Puerto Rico
  3. Cuba
   a. Problems
   b. Platt Amendment
   c. Guantanamo Bay

III. Rivalries in East Asia
  A. China
   1. Stagnant and weak
   2. Spheres of influence
   3. Open Door policy

  B. Boxer Rebellion

IV. Theodore Roosevelt's diplomacy
  A. Background to TR's presidency
   1. Election of 1900
    a. Referendum on imperialism
    b. McKinley wins
   2. McKinley's assassination
   3. TR's personal history

  B. The Panama Canal
   1. Negotiations with British and French
   2. Difficulties with Colombia
   3. Revolution in Panama
   4. Treaty with Panama
   5. Opening of canal

  C. The Roosevelt Corollary
   1. Problems of debt collection
   2. Principles in new policy

  D. TR's role in the Russo-Japanese War

  E. American relations with Japan
   1. Agreements on Korea, China, and Philippines
   2. Racism
   3. "Gentlemen's Agreement" of 1907

  F. The United States and Europe
   1. Conference at Algeciras
   2. Tour of the "Great White Fleet"

KEY ITEMS OF CHRONOLOGY

Purchase of Alaska	1867
Mahan's *Influence of Seapower upon History*	1890
de Lôme letter revealed	February 9, 1898
Maine sunk	February 15, 1898
War formally declared between Spain and the United States	April 1898
Hawaii annexed	July 1898
Armistice	August 1898
Treaty of Paris	December 1898
Anti-Imperialist League formed	1899
Open Door Note	1899
Assassination of McKinley	1901
Panama Canal acquired	1903
Roosevelt Corollary announced	1904
"Gentlemen's Agreement" with Japan	1907

TERMS TO MASTER

Listed below are some important terms or people with which you should be familiar after you complete the study of this chapter. Identify and explain each name or term.

1. Alfred Thayer Mahan
2. John Fiske
3. Josiah Strong
4. William H. Seward
5. yellow journalism
6. de Lôme letter
7. Teller Amendment
8. Platt Amendment
9. Open Door Policy
10. Boxer Rebellion
11. Panama Canal
12. Roosevelt Corollary
13. Portsmouth conference
14. "Gentlemen's Agreement"
15. "Great White fleet"

VOCABULARY BUILDING

Listed below are some words used in this chapter. Look in the dictionary for the meaning of each.

1. languid
2. bask
3. buffer
4. ordain
5. intertwine
6. burgeoning
7. subjugate
8. advocate (n.)
9. buttress (v.)
10. prevail
11. sanction
12. atoll
13. subsidy
14. muster
15. ambivalence
16. crescendo
17. armistice
18. insurrection
19. garrison
20. annex
21. sporadic
22. guerrilla
23. irksome
24. stagnant
25. pious
26. referendum
27. omnivorous
28. prodigious
29. boon
30. corollary

EXERCISES FOR UNDERSTANDING

When you have completed reading the chapter, answer each of the following questions. If you have difficulty, go back and reread the section of the chapter related to the question.

Multiple-Choice Questions

Select the letter of the response that best completes the statement.

1. The writings of Alfred Thayer Mahan on expansionism emphasized the
   A. ideas of Social Darwinism.
   B. importance of sea power.
   C. need for external markets.
   D. superiority of Anglo-Saxons.
2. William H. Seward was largely responsible for
   A. starting yellow journalism.
   B. developing the United States Navy.
   C. the sinking of the *Maine*.
   D. acquiring Alaska.
3. In the 1870s and 1880s, the nation's expansionists focused on
   A. Latin America.
   B. the Pacific Ocean.
   C. the Caribbean.
   D. Europe.
4. In 1893, the United States nearly annexed
   A. Hawaii.
   B. Cuba.
   C. Mexico.
   D. Hong Kong.
5. In 1898, the United States overcame its doubts about overseas possessions because it
   A. needed naval bases.
   B. wanted to expand commercial trade.

C. was outraged at Spanish imperialism.

D. wanted to spread Christianity.

6. The latest evidence suggests the sinking of the *Maine* was caused by
   A. jingoistic Americans.
   B. Cuban independence fighters to bring the United States into war.
   C. the Spanish to provoke war.
   D. an accidental fire on the ship.

7. An early and major victory in the Spanish-American War occurred at
   A. Algeciras.
   B. Santiago.
   C. Hawaii.
   D. Manila Bay.

8. During the Spanish-American War, Theodore Roosevelt fought in
   A. Hawaii.
   B. the Philippines.
   C. Cuba.
   D. Samoa.

9. The 1898 Treaty of Paris was opposed by most
   A. Populists.
   B. Democrats.
   C. anti-imperialists.
   D. all of the above

10. Independence for the Philippines came in
    A. 1900.
    B. 1906.
    C. 1916.
    D. 1946.

11. In 1901 the Platt Amendment
    A. granted the Philippines independence in 1916.
    B. provided that Hawaii would eventually become a state.
    C. gave the United States the right to intervene in Cuba.
    D. established a civilian government in Puerto Rico.

12. John Hay's Open Door Note of 1899 called for
    A. freedom for the Philippines and Hawaii.
    B. keeping trade with China open to all countries.
    C. increasing the immigration rate to the United States.
    D. annexation of Hawaii and Puerto Rico.

13. William Jennings Bryan wanted the 1900 presidential election to focus on
    A. imperialism.
    B. inflation and the money supply.
    C. the plight of farmers.
    D. the regulation of monopolies.

14. The United States obtained the right to build a canal across Panama after Panama got its independence from
    A. Spain.
    B. Colombia.
    C. Mexico.
    D. Great Britain.

15. The Roosevelt Corollary
    A. gave the United States police power in the Western Hemisphere.
    B. pledged American military force to maintain an "open door" in China.
    C. called for free elections in Japan after the Russo-Japanese War.
    D. denied United States interest in building a canal in Panama.

True-False Questions

Indicate whether each statement is true or false.

1. Western imperialism in the nineteenth century was primarily a drive for markets and raw materials.

2. Josiah Strong used religion to support imperialism.

3. As a result of the Spanish-American War, the United States annexed Hawaii in 1898.

4. Joseph Pulitzer's *New York World* engaged in "yellow journalism."

5. The United States entered war with Spain largely because American business interests demanded it.

6. The Teller Amendment called for annexation of Cuba.

7. Commodore George Dewey played a key role in the invasion of Cuba.

8. In the debate over the Treaty of Paris, the disposition of Cuba was the key issue.

9. William Jennings Bryan supported ratification of the Treaty of Paris.

10. The members of the Anti-Imperialist League generally were younger Americans.
11. The Foraker Act applied to Puerto Rico.
12. The Boxer Rebellion took place in China.
13. In 1901, Theodore Roosevelt was the youngest man to become president.
14. Theodore Roosevelt once served as police commissioner of New York City.
15. The United States sided with Russia in the Russo-Japanese War.

Essay Questions

1. What arguments did Americans use to justify imperialism, and how did the anti-imperialists rebut them?

2. Trace the key events leading up to the outbreak of the Spanish-American War.
3. What were the arguments favoring and opposing annexing territories after the Spanish-American War? Which argument made the most sense? Are the positions relevant today?
4. Explain the Open Door Policy and its effects.
5. How did the United States acquire the Panama Canal? Was it an example of imperialism?
6. What were Theodore Roosevelt's foreign policies? Do you think they were related to his personality?

ANSWERS TO MULTIPLE-CHOICE AND TRUE-FALSE QUESTIONS

Multiple-Choice Questions

1-B, 2-D, 3-B, 4-A, 5-C, 6-D, 7-D, 8-C, 9-D, 10-D, 11-C, 12-B, 13-A, 14-B, 15-A

True-False Questions

1-T, 2-T, 3-F, 4-T, 5-F, 6-F, 7-F, 8-F, 9-T, 10-F, 11-T, 12-T, 13-T, 14-T, 15-F

23 ∽

THE PROGRESSIVE ERA

CHAPTER OBJECTIVES

After you complete the reading and study of this chapter, you should be able to

1. Describe the nature and the goals of the progressive movement.
2. Compare the progressive movement with the populist movement.
3. Analyze Roosevelt's brand of progressivism.
4. Account for Taft's mixed record as a progressive.
5. Evaluate Wilson's efforts for progressive reform.
6. Assess the impact of progressivism on American politics, society, and economy.

CHAPTER OUTLINE

I. The nature of progressivism
  A. General features
    1. Aimed against the abuses of the Gilded-Age bosses
    2. Goals
      a. Greater democracy
      b. Honest, efficient government
      c. Effective business regulation
      d. Greater social justice

    3. A paradox of regulation of business by businessmen
    4. A diverse movement
  B. Antecedents
    1. Problems of industrialization and urbanization
    2. Urban reform
    3. Mugwumps
    4. Socialist critiques of living and working conditions
    5. Role of the muckrakers
      a. Exposing scandal
      b. Henry Demarest Lloyd and Lincoln Steffens
      c. Stronger on diagnosis than remedy
  C. The themes of progressivism
    1. Democratizing the government
      a. Direct primaries
      b. Initiative, referendum, recall
      c. Direct election of senators
    2. Efficiency and good government
      a. Frederick W. Taylor and scientific management
      b. Commission and city-manager forms of city government
      c. Use of specialists in government and business
        i. Robert M. La Follette

   ii. "Wisconsin Idea"
  3. Regulation of giant corporations
   a. Acceptance and regulation of big business
   b. Problem of regulating the regulators
  4. Impulse toward social justice
   a. Private charities and state power
   b. Outlawing child labor
   c. Erratic course of the Supreme Court
   d. Restricting working hours and dangerous occupations
   e. Stricter building codes and factory inspection acts
   f. Pressure for prohibition

II. Roosevelt's progressivism
 A. TR's expansive view
 B. Focus on trust regulation
  1. Opposition to wholesale trust-busting
  2. Northern Securities case (1904) used to promote the issue
  3. The "beef trust"
 C. Coal strike of 1902
  1. Basis for the UMW strike
  2. Recalcitrant attitude of management
  3. TR's efforts to force arbitration
  4. Effects of the incident
 D. Congressional action
  1. Department of Commerce and Labor
  2. Elkins Act
 E. Other antitrust suits

III. TR's second term
 A. Election of 1904
 B. Roosevelt's legislative leadership
  1. Hepburn Act
  2. Roosevelt's support of regulation of food and drugs
   a. Role of muckrakers
   b. Upton Sinclair and others
 C. Efforts for conservation
  1. Earlier movements for conservation
  2. Roosevelt's actions

IV. Taft's administration
 A. Selection of a successor in 1908
  1. TR's choice
  2. Democrats and Bryan
  3. Election results
 B. Taft's background and character
 C. Campaign for tariff reform
  1. Problems in Senate
  2. Taft's clash with the Progressive Republicans
 D. Ballinger-Pinchot controversy
 E. Roosevelt's response upon his return to the United States
  1. Initial silence
  2. Development of the New Nationalism
  3. TR enters the race
 F. Taft's achievements

V. The election of 1912
 A. The Republican nomination of 1912
 B. Creation of the Progressive party
 C. Wilson's rise to power
  1. His background
  2. Governor of New Jersey
  3. His nomination
 D. Focus of the campaign on the New Nationalism and the New Freedom
 E. Wilson's election
 F. Significance of the election of 1912
  1. High-water mark for progressivism
  2. Brought Democrats back into office
  3. Brought southerners into control

VI. Wilsonian reform
 A. Wilson's style
 B. Tariff reform
  1. Personal appearance before Congress
  2. Tariff changes in the Underwood-Simmons Act
  3. Income tax provisions
 C. The Federal Reserve Act
  1. Compromises required
  2. Description of the Federal Reserve System

D. Efforts for new antitrust laws
  1. Wilson's approach in 1912
  2. Federal Trade Commission Act
  3. Clayton Antitrust Act
     a. Practices outlawed
     b. Provisions for labor and farm organizations
  4. Disappointments with administration of the new laws
E. The shortcomings of Wilson's progressivism
  1. Women's suffrage
  2. Child labor
  3. Racist attitudes
F. Wilson's return to reform
  1. Plight of the Progressive party
  2. Appointment of Brandeis to the Supreme Court
  3. Support for land banks and long-term farm loans
  4. Farm demonstration agents and agricultural education
  5. Labor reform legislation
G. The paradoxes of progressivism

KEY ITEMS OF CHRONOLOGY

Wealth Against Commonwealth	1894
Roosevelt administration	1901–1909
Anthracite coal strike	1902
Shame of the Cities	1904
Northern Securities case	1904
Elkins Act	1903
Lochner v. *New York*	1905
Hepburn Act	1906
Pure Food and Drug Act	1906
Triangle Shirtwaist Company fire	1911
Supreme Court breaks up Standard Oil and American Tobacco Company	1911
Wilson administration	1913–1921
Sixteenth Amendment (income tax) ratified	1913
Seventeenth Amendment	1913
Underwood-Simmons Tariff Act	1913
Federal Reserve Act	1913
Federal Trade Commission Act	1914
Clayton Antitrust Act	1914
Adamson Act	1916

TERMS TO MASTER

Listed below are some important terms or people with which you should be familiar after you complete the study of this chapter. Identify and explain each name or term.

1. muckrakers
2. initiative and referendum
3. Frederick W. Taylor
4. Northern Securities case
5. anthracite coal strike
6. Robert M. La Follette
7. Elkins Act
8. Hepburn Act
9. Upton Sinclair's *Jungle*
10. Ballinger-Pinchot controversy
11. New Nationalism
12. New Freedom
13. Federal Reserve System
14. Federal Trade Commission
15. Clayton Antitrust Act

VOCABULARY BUILDING

Listed below are some words used in this chapter. Look up each word in the dictionary.

1. adroit
2. aloof
3. amalgam
4. bent (n.)
5. coalition
6. critique
7. demise
8. elicit
9. enact
10. erratic
11. exonerate
12. fermenting
13. fervor
14. festering
15. fruition
16. genteel
17. implicit
18. intricate
19. mandate
20. naive
21. plaudit
22. plight
23. prestige
24. prevalence
25. rebuke
26. salient
27. shoddily
28. slum
29. vehement
30. zenith

EXERCISES FOR UNDERSTANDING

When you have completed reading the chapter, answer each of the following questions. If you have difficulty, go back and reread the section of the chapter related to the question.

Multiple-Choice Questions

Select the letter of the response that best completes the statement.

1. Progressive reformers shared a belief in
   A. the virtues of small-scale enterprise.
   B. Protestant Christianity.
   C. the benefits of socialism.
   D. expanding governmental authority.
2. Lincoln Steffens and Henry Demarest Lloyd were examples of
   A. Mugwumps.
   B. muckrakers.
   C. "wooden-headed" businessmen.
   D. efficiency experts.
3. The popular election of United States senators resulted from
   A. *Lochner* v. *New York.*
   B. the Seventeenth Amendment.
   C. *E. C. Knight* v. *U.S.*
   D. the Hepburn Act of 1906.
4. Robert M. La Follette was the most important advocate of
   A. trust-busting.
   B. prohibition.
   C. experts in government.
   D. conservation of natural resources.
5. The most controversial issue at the turn of the century was
   A. imperialism.
   B. regulation of corporations.
   C. Americanization of new immigrants.
   D. the protection of women workers.
6. In two cases from Oregon (*Muller* and *Bunting*), the Supreme Court by 1917 had upheld laws
   A. setting minimum wages for industrial workers.
   B. eliminating industrial child labor.
   C. breaking up monopolies.
   D. limiting the workday to ten hours.
7. In *U.S.* v. *Northern Securities Company,* Roosevelt successfully broke up
   A. a railroad holding company.
   B. the beef trust.
   C. J. P. Morgan's dominance of Wall Street.
   D. the sugar trust.
8. The Interstate Commerce Commission got the power to set maximum railroad rates under the
   A. Sixteenth Amendment.
   B. Hepburn Act.
   C. Supreme Court's decision in the Northern Securities case.
   D. Sherman Antitrust Act.

9. Theodore Roosevelt was succeeded as president by
   A. William McKinley.
   B. William Howard Taft.
   C. Woodrow Wilson.
   D. Warren Harding.
10. Taft disappointed former president Roosevelt with his policies regarding
    A. tariff reform.
    B. antitrust.
    C. conservation.
    D. all of the above
11. In 1912, Roosevelt ran for president as a
    A. Progressive.
    B. Democrat.
    C. Republican.
    D. Socialist.
12. The tradition favoring antitrust action and decentralized government was represented in the 1912 election by
    A. Woodrow Wilson.
    B. Theodore Roosevelt.
    C. William Howard Taft.
    D. Eugene V. Debs.
13. The cornerstone of Wilson's antitrust program was the
    A. Clayton Act.
    B. Federal Trade Commission.
    C. Federal Reserve Act.
    D. Seventeenth Amendment.
14. Evidence that President Wilson became more progressive included his
    A. naming Louis Brandeis to the Supreme Court.
    B. support for farm credits.
    C. acceptance of child-labor legislation.
    D. all of the above
15. The Adamson Act of 1916 established
    A. the prohibition of alcoholic beverages.
    B. a program for agricultural education.
    C. a federal highway construction program.
    D. an eight-hour workday for railroad workers.

True-False Questions

Indicate whether each statement is true or false.

1. Some businessmen preferred government regulation to unrestrained competition.
2. The most important democratic reform by the progressives was the direct primary.
3. Frederick W. Taylor stressed the importance of social justice in the operation of factories.
4. The Wisconsin Idea involved protection of the family farm.
5. The fire at the Triangle Shirtwaist Company led to the abolition of child labor.
6. Progressive reformers gradually shifted from seeking to break up large corporations to wanting to regulate them.
7. In the anthracite coal strike of 1902, President Roosevelt used troops to keep the mines open.
8. In 1911, the Supreme Court broke up both Standard Oil and the American Tobacco Company.
9. Upton Sinclair's *Shame of the Cities* led to passage of the Meat Inspection Act.
10. Taft brought three times as many antitrust suits as had Roosevelt.
11. Roosevelt and Taft agreed in the Ballinger-Pinchot controversy.
12. Before running for president, Woodrow Wilson had been governor of Virginia.
13. As president, Wilson moved from the New Freedom toward the New Nationalism.
14. The federal income tax started in 1913 under Woodrow Wilson and the Sixteenth Amendment.
15. Under Wilson, racial segregation among federal employees increased.

Essay Questions

1. What forces led to the emergence of a progressive movement?
2. What were the four main features of progressive reform? What was a significant example of each?

3. Who were the candidates and what were the issues in the 1912 election? Why was it significant?

4. In what ways was William Howard Taft a successful president?

5. How did Woodrow Wilson's policies change between 1912 and 1917?

6. What were the limitations of progressivism? What were its lasting contributions?

ANSWERS TO MULTIPLE-CHOICE AND TRUE-FALSE QUESTIONS

Multiple-Choice Questions

1-D, 2-B, 3-B, 4-C, 5-B, 6-D, 7-A, 8-B, 9-B, 10-D, 11-A, 12-A, 13-B, 14-D, 15-D

True-False Questions

1-T, 2-T, 3-F, 4-F, 5-F, 6-T, 7-F, 8-T, 9-F, 10-T, 11-F, 12-F, 13-T, 14-T, 15-T

24 ∞

AMERICA AND THE GREAT WAR

CHAPTER OBJECTIVES

After you complete the reading and study of this chapter, you should be able to

1. Describe Wilson's idealistic diplomacy and show the clash of ideals and reality in Mexico.
2. Explain early United States reaction to the World War.
3. Trace the entry of the United States into World War I.
4. Evaluate the status of civil liberties during World War I and during the Red Scare afterward.
5. Explain the process and product of peacemaking after World War I.
6. Account for the failure of the United States to ratify the peace treaty after World War I.
7. Understand the problems of reconversion from World War I to civilian life.

CHAPTER OUTLINE

I. Wilson and foreign affairs
  A. Inexperience and idealism
  B. Intervention in Mexico
    1. Revolution
    2. Nonrecognition of the Huerta government
    3. Invasion at Veracruz
    4. Carranza's government
    5. The pursuit of Pancho Villa
  C. Problems in the Caribbean

II. America's uneasy neutrality
  A. Outbreak of the war
  B. Unprecedented war
    1. Scope of fighting
    2. Horrors of war
  C. Initial American response
    1. Declaration of neutrality
    2. Attitudes of immigrants
    3. Views of other American groups
    4. Effect of propaganda on Americans
  D. Extension of economic credit to the Allies
  E. Problems of neutrality
    1. Conflicts over neutral rights at sea
    2. German use of submarines
    3. Sinking of the *Lusitania*
      a. American protests
      b. Bryan's resignation
      c. *Arabic* pledge
  F. Debate over preparedness
    1. Demands for stronger army and navy
    2. National Defense Act of 1916
    3. Move for a stronger navy
    4. Revenue Act of 1916

G. Election of 1916
   1. Republicans nominated
   2. Democratic program
   3. Issues of the campaign
   4. Results of the election
H. Last efforts for peace
   1. Wilson's actions
   2. Germany's unrestricted submarine warfare
   3. Diplomatic break with Germany
   4. Bombshells of March 1917
     a. Zimmerman Telegram
     b. Russian Revolution

III. United States entry into the war
  A. Wilson's call for war
  B. Reasons for United States entry into the war
  C. America's early role
   1. Loans to allies
   2. Raising an army
  D. Mobilizing the home front
   1. Regulating the economy
     a. Government agencies
     b. War Industries Board
   2. Wartime labor force
     a. Blacks
     b. Mexican Americans
     c. Women
     d. Unions
  E. War propaganda and civil liberties in the war
   1. Committee on Public Information
   2. Popular disdain for all things German
   3. Espionage and Sedition Acts
     a. Terms of the acts
     b. Prosecutions
     c. Impact of the acts
     d. *Schenck* v. *United States*

IV. The American role in the war
  A. Allies' situation
  B. Western front
   1. German offensives

   2. American offensives
  C. Russian intervention
  D. The Fourteen Points
   1. Origins
   2. Content
   3. Purposes
   4. Responses
  E. Terms of the armistice

V. The fight for the peace
  A. Wilson's role
   1. Decision to attend the peace conference
   2. Effects of congressional elections of 1918
   3. Structure of the conference
  B. Emphasis on the League of Nations
   1. Article X of the charter
   2. Early warning from Lodge
  C. Concessions to French
  D. Compromises on national self-determination
  E. The agreement for reparations
  F. Obtaining the German signature
  G. Wilson's loss at home
   1. Support for the peace
   2. Lodge's reaction
   3. Opponents of the treaty
   4. Wilson's speaking tour
   5. Wilson's stroke
   6. Failure of the Senate votes
   7. Formal ending of the war

VI. Conversion to peace
  A. Spanish flu epidemic
  B. Labor unrest
  C. Race riots
  D. The Red Scare
   1. Fear of radicals
   2. Bombs in the mail
   3. Deportation of aliens
   4. Evaporation of the Red Scare
   5. Legacy of the Red Scare

KEY ITEMS OF CHRONOLOGY

Huerta in power in Mexico	February 1913
Invasion of Veracruz	April 1914

Outbreak of World War I	August 1914
Lusitania sunk	May 1915
Arabic pledge from Germany	September 1915
National Defense Act	1916
Wilson reelected	November 1916
Germany resumed unrestricted submarine warfare	February 1917
United States declared war	April 1917
Creation of War Industries Board	July 1917
Wilson announced Fourteen Points	January 1918
Treaty of Brest-Litovsk	March 1918
Armistice	November 1918
Spanish flu epidemic	1918
Paris Peace Conference	January–May 1919
Boston police strike	September 1919
Senate votes on treaty	November 1919 and March 1920
Red Scare	1919–1920

TERMS TO MASTER

Listed below are some important terms or people with which you should be familiar after you complete the study of this chapter. Identify and explain each name or term.

1. Victoriano Huerta
2. Pancho Villa
3. dollar diplomacy
4. Triple Alliance
5. Triple Entente
6. U-boat
7. *Lusitania*
8. *Arabic* pledge
9. preparedness
10. Revenue Act of 1916
11. Zimmerman Telegram
12. John J. Pershing
13. conscription
14. Food Administration
15. War Industries Board
16. Great Migration
17. Committee on Public Information
18. Espionage and Sedition Acts
19. *Schenck* v. *United States*
20. Treaty of Brest-Litovsk
21. Fourteen Points
22. Big Four
23. Henry Cabot Lodge
24. reparations
25. irreconcilables
26. League of Nations
27. Versailles Treaty
28. reservationists
29. Spanish flu

VOCABULARY BUILDING

Listed below are some words used in this chapter. Look up each word in the dictionary.

1. coup
2. embargo
3. spoils
4. incendiary
5. exalted
6. consortium
7. orgy
8. carnage
9. surrealistic
10. enmity
11. embodiment
12. attrition
13. ruse
14. disavow
15. crucible
16. belligerent
17. overt
18. envoy
19. exigency

20. mutiny
21. polarized
22. cynical
23. grouse (v.)
24. reparation
25. clamor
26. covenant
27. invalid
28. peevish
29. pandemic
30. liaison

EXERCISES FOR UNDERSTANDING

When you have completed the reading of the chapter, answer each of the following questions. If you have difficulty, go back and reread the section of the chapter related to the question.

Multiple-Choice Questions

Select the letter of the response that best completes the statement.

1. In dealing with the instability in Mexico, President Wilson
   A. sent troops ashore at Veracruz.
   B. refused to employ the military.
   C. consistently sided against Pancho Villa.
   D. received the enthusiastic support of Theodore Roosevelt.
2. American foreign policy in China and later in the Caribbean was called
   A. gunboat diplomacy.
   B. good neighbor diplomacy.
   C. dollar diplomacy.
   D. renegade intervention diplomacy.
3. As part of what was known as "Yankee imperialism," the United States had troops in
   A. Haiti from 1915 to 1934.
   B. Nicaragua from 1912 to 1933.
   C. the Dominican Republic from 1916 to 1924.
   D. all of the above
4. In World War I, the United States's allies,

the Triple Entente or Allied Powers, consisted of
   A. France, Great Britain, and Italy.
   B. Austria-Hungary and Great Britain.
   C. France, Great Britain, and Russia.
   D. Great Britain, Russia, and Italy.
5. In the propaganda war in World War I, one major advantage of the British was that
   A. most Americans did not speak German.
   B. all news from the battlefields came through London.
   C. their anti-Semitic propaganda appealed to many Americans.
   D. British radio broadcasts from Canada could reach the United States but German ones could not.
6. In the *Arabic* pledge,
   A. Germany pledged not to sink ships without warning and not to harm civilians.
   B. the United States promised to arm its passenger ships.
   C. Germany agreed not to use submarines in the Atlantic.
   D. the British declared unarmed German merchants ships would be sunk.
7. After the sinking of the *Lusitania*, William Jennings Bryan
   A. urged Wilson to declare war.
   B. resigned in protest over American demands on Germany.
   C. called for arming all passenger ships.
   D. campaigned for preparedness.
8. The Revenue Act of 1916
   A. taxed excess corporate profits.
   B. added a graduated estate tax.
   C. doubled the basic income tax.
   D. all of the above
9. The most important wartime government agency was the
   A. War Industries Board.
   B. Committee on Public Information.
   C. Food Administration.
   D. National Guard.
10. The Great Migration of the 1910s and 1920s involved
   A. civilians moving to areas around military bases.

B. second-generation immigrants moving to the West.

C. southern blacks moving northward.

D. the development of suburbs.

11. The Committee on Public Information was an example of

A. progressive efficiency.

B. propaganda.

C. "expression, not repression."

D. all of the above

12. In 1920, Eugene V. Debs received one million votes for president while he was

A. serving in the army in Europe.

B. a member of the Wilson administration.

C. in jail for encouraging draft resistance.

D. negotiating with Wilson at Versailles.

13. As a result of the Treaty of Brest-Litovsk,

A. Britain ended its fighting against Russia.

B. Germany agreed to stop submarine warfare.

C. the United States agreed to send troops to Europe.

D. Russia pulled out of the war.

14. The fourteenth of Wilson's Fourteen Points called for

A. freedom of the seas.

B. an open door policy in all of Europe.

C. a league of nations.

D. reparations by Germany and Italy.

15. Wilson's mistakes with the postwar settlement included

A. omitting Republicans from the negotiating team.

B. not campaigning for Democratic candidates in 1918.

C. compromising too readily with Henry Cabot Lodge.

D. all of the above

True-False Questions

Indicate whether each statement is true or false.

1. President Wilson supported General Huerta in Mexico after Huerta assumed power.

2. World War I started in Europe in August 1916.

3. At the time of World War I, more than a quarter of the United States population was first- or second-generation immigrants.

4. In the stalemated trench warfare of World War I, the British naval power played a very small role.

5. Both the British and the Germans violated neutral rights on the high seas.

6. When the *Lusitania* was sunk, more than one thousand people died, but none was American.

7. The Democrats' most popular issue in 1916 was neutrality.

8. The Zimmerman Telegram involved Wilson's efforts to keep the new Russian government involved in the war.

9. The United States entered World War I in April 1916.

10. To raise a large army, the United States resorted to conscription.

11. As a result of wartime mobilization, female long-term employment patterns changed very little.

12. In *Schenck* v. *United States,* Justice Oliver Wendell Holmes referred to "shouting fire in a theater" and the standard of "a clear and present danger."

13. Henry Cabot Lodge was an "irreconcilable" in the fight over the League of Nations.

14. The influenza epidemic of 1918-1919 killed 500,000 Americans.

15. A. Mitchell Palmer was attorney general during the Red Scare.

Essay Questions

1. How did Wilson apply his ideas and convictions in diplomacy with Mexico and the Caribbean?

2. How did the debate over the United States's entry into World War I resemble the postwar debate over the League of Nations?

3. What were the key events and decisions in the United States's shift from neutrality in 1914 to intervention in 1917?

4. How did the United States mobilize men, arms, and money for World War I?

5. Why didn't the United States join the League of Nations?

6. Was Wilson successful in leading the United States in foreign affairs?

7. How did civil liberties suffer during World War I and the years immediately after the war? How did the two periods differ?

ANSWERS TO MULTIPLE-CHOICE AND TRUE-FALSE QUESTIONS

Multiple-Choice Questions

1-A, 2-C, 3-D, 4-C, 5-B, 6-A, 7-B, 8-D, 9-A, 10-C, 11-D, 12-C, 13-D, 14-C, 15-A

True-False Questions

1-F, 2-F, 3-T, 4-F, 5-T, 6-F, 7-T, 8-F, 9-F, 10-T, 11-T, 12-T, 13-F, 14-T, 15-T

25 ∞

THE MODERN TEMPER

CHAPTER OBJECTIVES

After you complete the reading and study of this chapter, you should be able to

1. Describe and account for the mood of the 1920s.
2. Understand the nativist reaction in the twenties and the revival of the Ku Klux Klan, along with the consequences of these developments.
3. Trace the emergence of fundamentalism and its effects.
4. Account for the experiment in prohibition and its persistence in the face of widespread evasion of the law.
5. Describe and compare the political and social position of women and blacks in the twenties.
6. Explain the scientific basis of the moral relativism of the decade.
7. Assess the literary flowering of the 1920s and the contributions of major U.S. novelists and poets of the era.

CHAPTER OUTLINE

I. Reaction in the 1920s
   A. Changing moods

   1. Disillusionment
   2. Defiance against change
   B. Nativism
   1. Sacco and Vanzetti case
   2. Efforts to restrict immigration
   C. Revival of the Ku Klux Klan
   D. Fundamentalism
   1. Emergence of fundamentalism
   2. William Jennings Bryan
   3. Scopes trial
   E. Prohibition
   1. Reforming zeal
   2. Organization for the cause
   3. Constitutional amendment
   4. Organized crime and Al Capone
   5. Repeal

II. The Roaring Twenties
   A. A time of cultural conflict
   B. The Jazz Age
   1. Music
   2. Movies
   C. The new morality
   1. Emphasis on youth
   2. The "New Woman"
   3. Obsession with sex
   4. Impact of Freud
   5. Fashion
   D. The women's movement
   1. The work for women's suffrage

a. Alice Paul and new tactics
b. Contributions of Carrie Chapman Catt
c. Nineteenth Amendment
d. Effects of women's suffrage
2. Push for an Equal Rights Amendment
3. Women in the workforce
E. The "New Negro"
  1. The Great Migration north
    a. Demographics
    b. Impact of the move
  2. The Harlem Renaissance
  3. Marcus Garvey and Negro nationalism
    a. Universal Negro Improvement Association
    b. Separatism
  4. Development of the NAACP
    a. Emergence of the organization
    b. Role of Du Bois
    c. Strategy

d. The campaign against lynching
e. The Scottsboro case
III. The culture of modernism
  A. Science and social thought
    1. Einstein and the theory of relativity
    2. Uncertainty principle
    3. Denial of absolute values
  B. Modernist art and literature
    1. Bewildering technological change
    2. Characteristics
     a. Emphasis on subconscious
     b. Concern with new forms
    3. Prophets of modernism
     a. T. S. Eliot
     b. Ezra Pound
     c. Gertrude Stein
     d. F. Scott Fitzgerald
  C. Southern Renaissance
    1. Conflict of values
    2. William Faulkner

KEY ITEMS OF CHRONOLOGY

Einstein's paper on the Theory of Relativity	1905
Organization of the NAACP	1910
Ratification of the Eighteenth Amendment (prohibition)	1919
Ratification of the Nineteenth Amendment (women's suffrage)	1920
Sinclair Lewis's *Babbit*	1922
T. S. Eliot's *Wasteland*	1922
Scopes trial	1924
Execution of Sacco and Vanzetti	1927
Heisenberg's Principle of Uncertainty stated	1927
William Faulkner's *Sound and the Fury*	1929
Scottsboro case	1931

TERMS TO MASTER

Listed below are some important terms or people with which you should be familiar after you complete the study of this chapter. Identify or explain each.

1. Sacco and Vanzetti
2. KKK
3. fundamentalism
4. William Jennings Bryan
5. Clarence Darrow
6. "monkey trial"
7. Eighteenth Amendment
8. Al Capone
9. Jazz Age
10. Sigmund Freud

11. Alice Paul
12. Carrie Chapman Catt
13. Nineteenth Amendment
14. Great Migration
15. Harlem Renaissance
16. Marcus Garvey
17. NAACP
18. theory of relativity
19. modernist movement
20. Ezra Pound
21. T. S. Eliot
22. Gertrude Stein
23. F. Scott Fitzgerald
24. Southern Renaissance
25. William Faulkner

VOCABULARY BUILDING

Listed below are some words used in this chapter. Look up each word in the dictionary.

1. teeming
2. sedition
3. quota
4. ironic
5. horde
6. quarrel
7. schism
8. eloquence
9. evangelist
10. prescience
11. fatigue
12. zeal
13. bootlegging
14. lavishly
15. cosmopolitan
16. caricature
17. inane
18. banality
19. sublimation
20. doldrums
21. suffrage
22. ratification
23. bias
24. atrocity
25. filibuster
26. realms
27. ebb
28. atonal
29. exile
30. transmute

EXERCISES FOR UNDERSTANDING

When you have completed reading the chapter, answer each of the following questions. If you have difficulty, go back and reread the section of the chapter related to the question.

Multiple-Choice Questions

Select the letter of the response that best completes the statement.

1. The case of Sacco and Vanzetti was an example of
   A. nativism.
   B. modernism.
   C. existentialism.
   D. fundamentalism.
2. Immigration restriction legislation in the 1920s sought to
   A. reduce the total number of immigrants.
   B. prevent an influx of immigrants from Latin America and Asia.
   C. insure a greater percentage of immigrants from northern and western Europe.
   D. allow each country to send the same number of immigrants.
3. In the Scopes trial, Clarence Darrow was a(n)
   A. prosecutor.
   B. defense attorney.
   C. expert witness.
   D. interested observer.
4. Obstacles to prohibition included
   A. profits from bootlegging.
   B. inadequate congressional support for enforcement.
   C. public demand for alcohol.
   D. all of the above
5. An "experiment, noble in motive and far-reaching in purpose," is how Herbert Hoover described
   A. the League of Nations.
   B. women's suffrage.

C. modernism in literature.

D. prohibition.

6. The most popular form of mass culture in the 1920s was

A. radio.

B. baseball.

C. vaudeville.

D. movies.

7. Conservative moralists interpreted the flapper as an example of

A. moral degeneration.

B. rugged individualism.

C. Victorian morality.

D. the effects of fundamentalism.

8. In the 1920s after women got the vote, they

A. brought dramatic political change.

B. voted as men did.

C. spurred the women's movement to greater achievements.

D. overwhelmingly supported the Democratic party.

9. The most significant development in black life in the 1920s was the

A. Harlem Renaissance.

B. work of Marcus Garvey.

C. Great Migration northward.

D. campaign of the NAACP for equal rights.

10. Enforcement of the Fourteenth Amendment was stressed by

A. the NAACP.

B. Marcus Garvey.

C. the Harlem Renaissance.

D. the Ku Klux Klan.

11. The theory of relativity was devised by

A. Isaac Newton.

B. Albert Einstein.

C. Max Planck.

D. Werner Heisenberg.

12. William Faulkner was part of the

A. Harlem Renaissance.

B. "lost" generation.

C. Southern Renaissance.

D. all of the above

True-False Questions

Indicate whether each statement is true or false.

1. The Ku Klux Klan thrived only in the South.

2. Fundamentalism was grounded in a belief in the literal truth of the Bible.

3. John Thomas Scopes was convicted at his trial in Dayton, Tennessee.

4. The Eighteenth Amendment banned the consumption of intoxicating liquors.

5. The Nineteenth Amendment gave women the right to vote.

6. Carrie Chapman Catt was part of the Harlem Renaissance.

7. Claude McKay was the leader of the United Negro Improvement Association.

8. The Harlem Renaissance was a political movement centered in New York City.

9. In 1922, Congress enacted an anti-lynching law.

10. Innovations in the laws of physics undermined belief in personal responsibility and absolute standards.

11. The chief American prophets of modernism lived in New York City.

12. American writers living in Paris in the 1920s became known as the "lost" generation.

Essay Questions

1. What were the reactionary forces at work in society in the 1920s?

2. In what way were the 1920s "roaring"?

3. Did Marcus Garvey or the Harlem Renaissance have the greater impact on black life in the 1920s?

4. How did scientific thinking affect social and literary values?

5. What was distinctly "modern" about some of the literature after World War I?

ANSWERS TO MULTIPLE-CHOICE AND TRUE-FALSE QUESTIONS

Multiple-Choice Questions

1-A, 2-C, 3-B, 4-D, 5-D, 6-D, 7-A, 8-B, 9-C, 10-A, 11-B, 12-C

True-False Questions

1-F, 2-T, 3-T, 4-T, 5-T, 6-F, 7-F, 8-F, 9-F, 10-T, 11-F, 12-T

26

REPUBLICAN RESURGENCE
AND DECLINE

CHAPTER OBJECTIVES

After you complete the reading and study of this chapter, you should be able to

1. Assess the effects of the Harding presidency on the nation.
2. Explain the new prosperity of the 1920s.
3. Describe the features of the economy in the New Era decade, especially the consumer culture.
4. Identify Hoover's policies for the nation and indicate their effects.
5. Account for the stock market crash of 1929.
6. Describe the status of farmers during the 1920s.
7. Discuss the status of labor unions during the 1920s.

CHAPTER OUTLINE

I. Progressivism in the twenties
   A. Dissolution of the progressive coalition in Congress
   B. Survivals of progressivism in the twenties

II. Normalcy
   A. Election of 1920

     1. Mood of the country
     2. Nomination of Harding
     3. Democratic candidate
     4. Results
   B. The Harding administration
     1. Appointments
     2. Policies
       a. Not progressive
       b. Pro-business
         i. Tax cuts
         ii. High tariff
         iii. War debts
         iv. Regulation
     3. Corruption
       a. Veterans Bureau
       b. Harry Daugherty
       c. Teapot Dome
       d. Harding's role
     4. Harding's death
     5. Assessment
   C. Calvin Coolidge
     1. Character
     2. Ideology
   D. Election of 1924
     1. Coolidge
     2. Democrats
     3. Results

III. The New Era
   A. Consumer culture
     1. Consumption ethic

2. Mass advertising
3. Communications
    a. Movies
    b. Radio
    c. National culture
4. Transportation
    a. Aviation
        i. Lindbergh
        ii. Earhart
    b. Automobiles
B. Republican economic policies
    1. Herbert Hoover's Commerce
        Department
    2. Trade associations
C. Agriculture
    1. Problems in agriculture
    2. Mechanization
    3. Marketing cooperatives
    4. Congressional action
        a. Farm bloc
        b. McNary-Haugen plan
D. Organized labor
    1. Earnings in industry
    2. Unions' setbacks
        a. Effects of Red Scare
        b. Employers' methods

IV. Hoover presidency
A. The election of 1928
    1. Candidates
    2. Issues
    3. Results

B. Hoover's initial policies
    1. Progressivism
    2. Sympathy for farmers
    3. Tariff reform
C. Problems with the economy
    1. Misguided optimism
    2. Collapse of Florida real estate
    3. Wall Street speculation
D. The crash
    1. October 29, 1929
    2. Effects on incomes and banks
    3. Causes
        a. Unsound business
        b. Governmental policies
        c. Gold standard
E. Human toll of depression
F. Hoover's responses
    1. Urge confidence
    2. Public building projects
    3. Ease credit
    4. Moratorium on reparations and
        war debts
G. Congressional actions
    1. Reconstruction Finance
        Corporation
    2. Glass-Steagall Act
    3. Federal Home Loan Bank Act
    4. Call for relief efforts
H. Protests by veterans and farmers
    1. Farmers' desperation
    2. Bonus Expeditionary Force
I. Mood of the nation

KEY ITEMS OF CHRONOLOGY

Model T Ford appeared	1908
Eighteenth Amendment	1919
Nineteenth Amendment	1920
Fordney-McCumber Tariff	1922
First radio commercial	1922
Death of Harding	1923
Florida real estate collapse	1926
Lindbergh flight	May 1927
McNary-Haugen bills passed by Congress	1927, 1928
Stock market crash	October 1929
Agricultural Marketing Act	1929
Smoot-Hawley Tariff	1930
Hoover's moratorium on war-debt payments	1931

Amelia Earhart flew the Atlantic	1931
Glass-Steagall Act	1932
Creation of Reconstruction Finance Corporation	1932
Attack on the Bonus Expeditionary Force	July 1932

TERMS TO MASTER

Listed below are some important terms or people with which you should be familiar after you complete the study of this chapter. Identify and explain each name or term.

1. Warren Harding
2. "normalcy"
3. "Ohio Gang"
4. Harry M. Daughtery
5. Andrew Mellon
6. Fordney-McCumber Tariff
7. Teapot Dome affair
8. Robert M. La Follette
9. Calvin Coolidge
10. Charles A. Lindbergh
11. Amelia Earhart
12. Herbert Hoover
13. associationalism
14. marketing cooperatives
15. McNary-Haugen plan
16. "yellow dog" contract
17. welfare capitalism
18. Alfred E. Smith
19. Agricultural Marketing Act
20. Smoot-Hawley Tariff
21. margin buying
22. Reconstruction Finance Corporation
23. Federal Home Loan Bank Act
24. Bonus Expeditionary Force
25. Glass-Steagall Act

VOCABULARY BUILDING

Listed below are some words used in this chapter. Look up each word in the dictionary.

1. fissure
2. erode
3. crusader
4. injunction

5. behest
6. lenient
7. corrupt
8. amorous
9. turmoil
10. rustic
11. evoke
12. creed
13. exult
14. vindication
15. havoc
16. frugality
17. eradicate
18. therapeutic
19. commodity
20. exempt (v.)
21. retrospect
22. subversion
23. coercion
24. tersely
25. hinterlands
26. exacerbate
27. flounder (v.)
28. destitute
29. shantytown
30. melee

EXERCISES FOR UNDERSTANDING

When you have completed reading the chapter, answer each of the following questions. If you have difficulty, go back and reread the section of the chapter related to the question.

Multiple-Choice Questions

Select the letter of the response that best completes the statement.

1. Progressivism's final triumphs included the
   A. election of Warren Harding in 1920.

B. enactment of the Fordney-McCumber Tariff in 1922.

C. passage of the Nineteenth Amendment.

D. defeat of the McNary-Haugen plan.

2. Harding's "Ohio Gang" included
   A. Herbert Hoover.
   B. Harry M. Daughtery.
   C. Charles Evans Hughes.
   D. Henry A. Wallace.

3. As Secretary of the Treasury, Andrew Mellon favored
   A. tax and spending cuts.
   B. lower tariffs.
   C. stricter regulation of business.
   D. stronger labor unions.

4. The Teapot Dome scandal involved
   A. federal land in Wyoming.
   B. German assets seized during the war.
   C. Harding's extramarital affairs.
   D. thefts from the Veterans Bureau.

5. "The chief business of the American people is business," declared
   A. Warren Harding.
   B. Herbert Hoover.
   C. Andrew Mellon.
   D. Calvin Coolidge.

6. More efficient industrial production in the 1920s required
   A. highly organized labor unions.
   B. stronger government regulation of industry.
   C. more widespread consumption.
   D. a large standing army.

7. As secretary of commerce, Herbert Hoover promoted
   A. standardization of products.
   B. free competition among businesses.
   C. the formation of monopolies.
   D. all of the above

8. During the 1920s, the weakest sector of the economy was
   A. aviation.
   B. the advertising industry.
   C. the steel industry.
   D. agriculture.

9. In the 1920s, McNary-Haugen bills sought to eliminate
   A. small businesses.
   B. surplus farm commodities.

C. speculation in the stock market.

D. unfair competition between railroads and airlines.

10. "Yellow-dog" contracts forced workers to
    A. vote for Democrats.
    B. join unions.
    C. stay out of unions.
    D. oppose welfare capitalism.

11. The Reconstruction Finance Corporation originally used $500 million to provide loans to
    A. individual homeowners.
    B. banks, railroads, and insurance companies.
    C. local municipal governments.
    D. all of the above

12. The Bonus Expeditionary Force
    A. consisted mainly of communists.
    B. used military force to make Congress act during the depression.
    C. wanted money promised to World War I veterans.
    D. sought a radical change in the nation's economy.

True-False Questions

Indicate whether each statement is true or false.

1. Franklin D. Roosevelt ran for vice president in 1920.

2. Harding appointed William Howard Taft to the Supreme Court.

3. Calvin Coolidge was directly involved in the Teapot Dome scandal.

4. Frugality, savings, and plain living were antithetical to the consumer culture of the 1920s.

5. The fastest growing part of the consumer culture in the 1920s was the movie industry.

6. In 1931, Charles Lindbergh flew across the Atlantic alone.

7. Herbert Hoover favored the establishment of trade associations.

8. Southern Democrats and western Republicans formed the farm bloc in congress.

9. The fundamental problem in agriculture in the 1920s was a lack of mechanization.
10. In the 1928 presidential election, Herbert Hoover defeated Al Smith.
11. Between 1929 and 1932, Americans' personal incomes actually increased.
12. The stock market crashed in October 1929.

Essay Questions

1. Which of the three Republican presidents in the 1920s was the most successful and which the least? Explain.
2. What was the new "consumer culture" and what led to its emergence?
3. Were the 1920s prosperous? Why or why not?
4. What caused the stock market crash and the Great Depression?
5. How did the depression affect ordinary Americans?
6. How did President Hoover respond to the economic crisis of 1929–33, and how did his efforts resemble his earlier policies?

ANSWERS TO MULTIPLE-CHOICE AND TRUE-FALSE QUESTIONS

Multiple-Choice Questions

1-C, 2-B, 3-A, 4-A, 5-D, 6-C, 7-A, 8-D, 9-B, 10-B, 11-B, 12-C

True-False Questions

1-T, 2-T, 3-F, 4-T, 5-F, 6-F, 7-T, 8-T, 9-F, 10-T, 11-F, 12-T

27

NEW DEAL AMERICA

CHAPTER OBJECTIVES

After you complete the reading and study of this chapter, you should be able to

1. Describe the character and appeal of FDR.
2. Describe the sources for New Deal legislation.
3. Explain the New Deal approaches to the problems of recovery in industry and agriculture.
4. Describe the criticisms made of the New Deal by the left and the right.
5. Describe New Deal efforts to deal with unemployment and welfare.
6. Assess the changes in the United States wrought by the New Deal.
7. Understand the outpouring of literature of social significance during the 1930s.

CHAPTER OUTLINE

I. From Hooverism to the New Deal
   A. Election of 1932
      1. Roosevelt
         a. Background
         b. Personality
         c. Health
      2. Campaign
      3. Hoover

   4. Result
   B. Inauguration
      1. Banking crisis
      2. Spirit of assurance
   C. Competing solutions
      1. Brain trust
      2. Options
         a. Antitrust action
         b. Collaborate with big business
         c. Government spending
      3. FDR's vacillating positions
   D. Strengthening financial institutions
      1. Bank holiday
      2. Banking legislation
      3. Securities Exchange Commission
      4. End of gold standard
   E. Relief measures
      1. Civilian Conservation Corps (CCC)
      2. Federal Emergency Relief Administration (FERA)
      3. Civil Works Administration (CWA)
      4. Works Progress Administration (WPA)

II. Recovery through regulation
    A. Aid for agriculture
       1. Agricultural Adjustment Administration (AAA)
       2. Commodity Credit Corporation

3. Effects on prices and production
4. *U.S.* v. *Butler*
5. Soil conservation
6. Second AAA
   B. Industrial recovery
   1. National Industrial Recovery Act (NIRA)
   2. Public Works Administration (PWA)
   3. National Recovery Administration (NRA)
      a. Objectives
      b. Fair practice codes
      c. Effects on labor
      d. Controversies
      e. Unconstitutional
   C. Tennessee Valley Authority (TVA)
   1. Background
   2. Purposes

III. The human cost of the depression
   A. Hardships in personal lives
   1. Unemployment
   2. Marriage and birthrates
   B. Dust bowl migrants
   1. Origins
   2. Destinations
   3. Okie subculture
   C. Minorities
   1. Programs for whites only
   2. Effects of crop reductions on tenants
   3. Mexican Americans
      a. Lack of citizenship
      b. Calls for deportation
   4. Native Americans
      a. John Collier
      b. Indian Reorganization Act

IV. Culture in the thirties
   A. Literature and the depression
   1. Effects of depression
      a. Social activism
      b. Communism
   2. Novelists of social significance
      a. John Steinbeck
      b. Richard Wright
   B. Popular culture
   1. Radio
      a. Entertainment
      b. Fireside chats

2. Movies
V. The Second New Deal
   A. Eleanor Roosevelt
   1. Background
   2. Role in administration
   B. Criticism of the New Deal
   1. American Liberty League
   2. Critics on the left
      a. Huey P. Long
      b. Francis E. Townsend
      c. Charles E. Coughlin
   3. Supreme Court
   C. Legislative achievements
   1. Wagner Act
   2. Social Security Act
      a. Pension fund
      b. Unemployment insurance
      c. Aid to unemployables
   3. Revenue Act of 1935

VI. FDR's second term
   A. Election of 1936
   1. Alfred M. Landon
   2. Union Party
   3. FDR's coalition
   4. Outcome
   B. Court-packing plan
   1. Enlarge the court
   2. Opposition
   3. Changes in the court
   4. Effects of fight
   C. Changes in labor
   1. Renewed unionization
   2. Rise of industrial unions
      a. Committee for Industrial Organization
      b. Split with American Federation of Labor
      c. Auto and steel workers
      d. Failure in the South
   D. Economic downturn
   1. 1937 slump
   2. Debate over policy
   3. Large-scale spending
   4. Decline in FDR's prestige
   E. Post-1936 reforms
   1. Wagner-Steagall National Housing Act
   2. Bankhead-Jones Farm Tenant Act
   3. Fair Labor Standards Act

F. Setbacks for Roosevelt
  1. Anti-New Deal bloc
  2. Anti-Communist crusade
  3. 1938 purge attempt

VII. Legacy of the New Deal: a halfway revolution
  A. Enlarged government
  B. Restoration of hope
  C. Increased government responsibility
  D. Revolutionary and conservative

KEY ITEMS OF CHRONOLOGY

FDR contracts polio	1921
Bonus Army march	1932
Roosevelt's administrations	1933–April 1945
The Hundred Days	March 4–June 16, 1933
Twentieth Amendment	1933
Federal Deposit Insurance Corporation created	1933
National Industrial Recovery Act	1933
Tennessee Valley Authority created	May 1933
Indian Reorganization Act passed	1934
Second New Deal initiatives	1935
Wagner Act passed	July 1935
Social Security started	August 1935
United States v. *Butler*	1936
AFL expelled CIO	1936
Court-packing plan presented	1937
The Grapes of Wrath	1939
Gone with the Wind	1939
Native Son	1940

TERMS TO MASTER

Listed below are some important terms or people with which you should be familiar after you complete the study of this chapter. Identify and explain each name or term.

1. brain trust
2. fireside chat
3. Hundred Days
4. Securities and Exchange Commission
5. Civilian Conservation Corps
6. Harry Hopkins
7. Works Progress Administration
8. Agricultural Adjustment Administration
9. processing tax
10. Dust Bowl
11. *United States* v. *Butler*
12. Soil Conservation Act
13. National Industrial Recovery Act (NIRA)
14. Public Works Administration
15. National Recovery Administration (NRA)
16. Tennessee Valley Authority
17. Rural Electrification Administration (REA)
18. Okies
19. Richard Wright
20. Eleanor Roosevelt
21. American Liberty League
22. Huey P. Long
23. Francis Townsend
24. Father Charles Coughlin
25. *Schechter Poultry Corp.* v. *United States*
26. Wagner Act
27. Social Security Act
28. court-packing plan
29. CIO
30. John L. Lewis

31. sit-down strike
32. Fair Labor Standards Act
33. broker state
34. modernism

VOCABULARY BUILDING

Listed below are some words used in this chapter. Look up each word in the dictionary.

1. affinity
2. penchant
3. affable
4. requisite
5. incur
6. ambiguous
7. distraught
8. infusion
9. vacillate
10. stringent
11. poignantly
12. throes
13. diluted
14. ghetto
15. egalitarian
16. carping
17. huckster
18. panacea
19. flamboyant
20. bumpkin
21. confiscate
22. galvanize
23. entail
24. contingent
25. forlorn
26. precedent
27. brazen
28. veneration
29. impetus
30. stymie

EXERCISES FOR UNDERSTANDING

When you have completed reading the chapter, answer each of the following questions. If you have difficulty, go back and reread the section of the chapter related to the question.

Multiple-Choice Questions

Select the letter of the response that best completes the statement.

1. Major restrictions on FDR's action in 1933 included
   A. southern Democratic control of congressional committees.
   B. general reluctance of the people for drastic action.
   C. his narrow victory margin.
   D. all of the above
2. On his first day in office, FDR
   A. had a fireside chat with the people.
   B. declared a bank holiday.
   C. endorsed prohibition.
   D. mobilized the army.
3. The second most powerful figure in the Roosevelt administration was
   A. Eleanor Roosevelt.
   B. Hugh S. Johnson.
   C. Huey P. Long.
   D. Harry L. Hopkins.
4. The first large-scale federal work relief program was the
   A. Civilian Conservation Corps.
   B. Tennessee Valley Authority.
   C. Works Progress Administration.
   D. Civil Works Administration.
5. The AAA sought to
   A. raise farm prices by cutting production.
   B. eliminate inefficient farmers.
   C. increase farm income by buying agricultural surpluses.
   D. have farmers shift from crops to cattle.
6. In *United States* v. *Butler,* the Supreme Court overturned the
   A. bank holiday.
   B. Civilian Conservation Corps.
   C. first AAA.
   D. Eighteenth Amendment.
7. Section 7a of the NIRA
   A. called for codes of fair practice in business.
   B. allocated $3.3 billion dollars for federal construction.
   C. guaranteed workers the right to form unions.
   D. prohibited price-fixing by corporations.

8. The New Deal's boldest experiment was
   A. Social Security.
   B. requiring farmers to plow up their crops.
   C. integration of the armed forces.
   D. the Tennessee Valley Authority.
9. During the 1930s, the
   A. divorce rate dropped.
   B. marriage rate fell.
   C. birthrate declined.
   D. all of the above
10. Conservative critics of the New Deal organized the
   A. Union party.
   B. Townsend movement.
   C. American Liberty League.
   D. Share Our Wealth Program.
11. The Supreme Court ruled unconstitutional
   A. the NIRA and the AAA.
   B. Social Security and the NIRA.
   C. TVA and AAA.
   D. the Wagner Act and the NIRA.
12. According to FDR, the "cornerstone" and "supreme achievement" of the New Deal was
   A. the TVA.
   B. the Wagner Act.
   C. Social Security.
   D. the PWA and WPA.
13. The court-packing plan was defeated in part because of
   A. Democratic losses in 1936.
   B. its violation of the Constitution.
   C. a change of direction by the court.
   D. all of the above
14. The Committee for Industrial Organizations worked hardest to organize workers in
   A. textiles and steel.
   B. autos and mining.
   C. mining and steel.
   D. autos and steel.
15. The Fair Labor Standards Act
   A. set a minimum wage for workers.
   B. limited the hours for workers.
   C. prohibited child labor.
   D. all of the above

True-False Questions

Indicate whether each statement is true or false.

1. In his 1932 campaign, FDR spelled out in detail what the New Deal would include.
2. By March 1933, four-fifths of the nation's banks had closed.
3. One early accomplishment of the New Deal was the creation of the Securities and Exchange Commission.
4. The Civilian Conservation Corps assisted men eighteen to twenty-five years old.
5. The "dust bowl" played a major role in cutting agricultural production.
6. The Roosevelt administration modeled the NRA after the War Industries Board of World War I.
7. The TVA involved electric power generation, conservation, and industrial development.
8. Richard Wright's *Native Son* was set in Oklahoma and California.
9. Huey Long was a senator from Michigan.
10. The Wagner Act outlawed child labor.
11. The Roosevelt coalition was forged in the 1936 election.
12. Father Charles Coughlin had a wider following than either Huey Long or Francis Townsend.
13. The Wealth Tax was the last major legislation of the "Second New Deal."
14. Steel workers originated the "sit-down strike" in 1937.
15. In 1937, the economy experienced significant economic growth for the first time since 1931.

A Match of New Deal Agencies

The New Deal period witnessed the creation of a plethora of new government agencies that became known as the alphabet agencies because they were referred to by their initials. To help you focus on major agencies and to test your grasp of the material, match the description or statement on the right with the agencies or act on the left below. Some of the agencies or acts may match with more than one description. Answers are at the end of this chapter.

Agency or Act	Description
1. FDIC	a. created a regional rehabilitation of a river basin
2. FERA	b. investigated the concentration of economic power in the United States
3. Economy Act	c. set minimum wages and maximum hours for certain industries in interstate commerce
4. First AAA	d. provided a variety of methods for increasing farm income
5. Civilian Conservation Corps	e. provided insurance for bank deposits
6. PWA	f. $3.3 billion for jobs on major building projects
7. TVA	g. a stopgap plan for aiding the unemployed in 1933–1935
8. NRA	h. loans to rural cooperatives to run electrical lines to remote farms
9. REA	i. a plan to cut wages of veterans and federal employees
10. Wagner Act	j. jobs for young men in the nation's parks
11. Social Security Act	k. an agency to regulate the sale of stocks and bonds
12. Wealth Tax Act	l. allowed industries to collaborate together to limit production of goods and raise wages
13. SEC	m. provided farmers payments to conserve soil by not planting crops
14. TNEC	n. created a committee to oversee elections for unions
15. Farm Security Administration	o. established the welfare system for mothers and dependent children
16. Soil Conservation Act	p. greatly increased income taxes
17. Fair Labor Standards Act	q. provided a tax on incomes to ensure retirement benefits
18. WPA	r. placed a tax on farm products when first processed for market
	s. provided loans to help farm tenants buy their land
	t. a long-term federal program to provide jobs, including symphony, artistic, and theater projects
	u. provided states aid for work projects as well as a dole
	v. built dams to produce and sell electricity
	w. a counterpart to NRA, this agency provided jobs on major construction projects

Essay Questions

1. How did the New Deal's programs for industry differ from its efforts to help farmers?
2. What were the major criticisms of the New Deal, from the left and the right?
3. How did the New Deal's approach change over time?
4. In what ways did the New Deal expand the authority and role of the federal government?
5. Why did the New Deal decline in the late 1930s?
6. What is the long-term significance of FDR and the New Deal?

ANSWERS TO MULTIPLE-CHOICE, TRUE-FALSE, AND MATCHING QUESTIONS

Multiple-Choice Questions

1-A, 2-B, 3-D, 4-D, 5-A, 6-C, 7-C, 8-D, 9-D, 10-C, 11-A, 12-C, 13-C, 14-D, 15-D

True-False Questions

1-F, 2-T, 3-T, 4-T, 5-T, 6-T, 7-T, 8-F, 9-F, 10-F, 11-T, 12-F, 13-T, 14-F, 15-F

Matching Questions

1-e, 2-q,u, 3-i, 4-d,r, 5-j, 6-f,w, 7-a,v, 8-l, 9-h, 10-n, 11-o,q, 12-p, 13-k, 14-b, 15-s, 16-m, 17-c, 18-t

28 ∞

FROM ISOLATION TO GLOBAL WAR

CHAPTER OBJECTIVES

After you complete the reading and study of this chapter, you should be able to

1. Explain and account for the foreign policy pursued by the United States in the interwar period.
2. Describe the aggressions of Japan, Italy, and Germany in the decade of the 1930s.
3. Account for American efforts at neutrality in the face of aggression and assess the effectiveness of neutrality in preventing war.
4. Describe the election of 1940.
5. Understand American support of Britain and the Soviet Union prior to the United States's entry into the war.
6. Explain and account for the effectiveness of the attack on Pearl Harbor.

CHAPTER OUTLINE

I. Postwar isolationism
   A. Evidence of isolationist sentiment
   B. Counteractions of world involvement
   C. Relations with the League
   D. Efforts toward disarmament
      1. A substitute for League membership

2. Strained Japanese-American relations
3. The Washington Armaments Conference
   a. Hughes's initiative
   b. Agreements made at the conference
   c. Effects of the treaties
4. The movement to outlaw war
   a. Development of the Kellogg-Briand Pact
   b. Effect of the pact
   E. The "good neighbor" policy
      1. Early efforts to improve relations with Latin America
      2. Hoover and the Clark Memorandum
      3. Further improvements under FDR

II. War clouds
   A. Japanese incursion in China
      1. Chinese weaknesses
      2. Japanese occupation of Manchuria
      3. Reactions to occupation
         a. League condemnation
         b. Japan's withdrawal from the League
   B. Mussolini's rise to power
   C. Hitler's rise to power

D. American recognition of the Soviet
   Union
E. Aggression in Asia and Europe
   1. Italian invasion of Ethiopia, 1935
   2. Hitler's occupation of the
      Rhineland, 1936
   3. Spanish Civil War, 1936
   4. Japanese invasion of China, 1937
   5. Hitler's *Anschluss* with Austria,
      1938
   6. The Munich Agreement, 1938
   7. War begun over Poland, 1939

III. American efforts for neutrality
   A. The Nye Committee investigations
   B. Congressional effort to avoid another
      world war
   C. The first Neutrality Act, 1935
      1. Sale of arms to belligerents
         forbidden
      2. Travel on belligerents' ships
         discouraged
   D. Reaction to the invasion of Ethiopia
   E. The second Neutrality Act: loans to
      belligerents forbidden
   F. Extension of the Neutrality Act to
      cover civil wars
   G. Further neutrality provisions
   H. Reactions to Japanese action in
      China
      1. Lack of use of neutrality laws
      2. Quarantine speech
   I. Reactions to war in Europe
      1. Change to cash-and-carry arms
         sales
      2. Extension of war zone

IV. The storm in Europe
   A. Hitler's *Blitzkrieg*
   B. American aid to embattled Britain
      1. Growth of U.S. defense effort
      2. Sales of arms to Britain
   C. Other defense measures
   D. The destroyer-bases deal
   E. Peacetime conscription
   F. Polarization of public opinion
      1. Committee to Defend America
      2. America First Committee

V. The election of 1940
   A. The choice of Willkie
   B. The choice of FDR
   C. Nature of the campaign
   D. Results of the election

VI. The arsenal of democracy
   A. The Lend-Lease program
   B. Reaction to the invasion of the Soviet
      Union
   C. The Atlantic Charter
   D. Conflict with the Germans in the
      Atlantic

VII. The storm in the Pacific
   A. Tripartite Pact
   B. Negotiations between Japan and the
      United States
   C. Warlords gain control in Japan
   D. Attack on Pearl Harbor
      1. Extent of U.S. foreknowledge
      2. Errors in warning
      3. Damage from the attack
      4. Other Japanese aggression in the
         Pacific
   E. Declaration of war

KEY ITEMS OF CHRONOLOGY

Washington Armaments Conference	1921–1922
Mussolini took power in Italy	1925
Kellogg-Briand Pact	1928
Japanese invasion of Manchuria	1931
Hitler took power in Germany	1933
London Economic Conference	1933
Nye Committee	1934–1937
Italy's invasion of Ethiopia	1935
Japan's invasion of China	1937
Quarantine Speech	1937

World War II begins	September 1, 1939
First peacetime draft	1940
Fall of France	June 1940
Lend-Lease program began	1941
Germany's invasion of Soviet Union	June 1941
Japanese extend protectorate over Indochina	July 1941
Attack on Pearl Harbor	December 7, 1941

TERMS TO MASTER

Listed below are some important terms or people with which you should be familiar after you complete the study of this chapter. Identify or explain each.

1. World Court
2. Washington Armaments Conference
3. isolationism
4. Five-Power Treaty
5. Kellogg-Briand Pact
6. Clark Memorandum
7. "good neighbor" policy
8. Nye Committee
9. "merchants of death"
10. Neutrality Acts
11. cash-and-carry
12. *Blitzkrieg*
13. America First Committee
14. Wendell Willkie
15. Lend-Lease program
16. Four Freedoms
17. Atlantic Charter

10. incursion
11. ludicrous
12. insularity
13. commissar
14. abstain
15. appease
16. fascist
17. reconvene
18. quarantine
19. illusion
20. swastika
21. conscription
22. quadrennial
23. default
24. invincibility
25. tripartite
26. protectorate
27. flank
28. imminent
29. fortuitously
30. infamy

VOCABULARY BUILDING

Listed below are some words used in this chapter. Look in the dictionary for the meaning of each.

1. volatile
2. relish (v.)
3. viscount
4. forestall
5. refrain (v.)
6. culminate
7. recourse
8. repudiate
9. abrogate

EXERCISES FOR UNDERSTANDING

When you have completed reading the chapter, answer each of the following questions. If you have difficulty, go back and reread the section of the chapter related to the question.

Multiple-Choice Questions

Select the letter of the response that best completes the statement.

1. The United States's interest in disarmament was prompted partially by a concern about the increasing power of
   A. Great Britain.

B. China.
C. Japan.
D. Germany.

2. The "way to disarm is to disarm," said
   A. Woodrow Wilson.
   B. Charles Evans Hughes.
   C. Warren Harding.
   D. Frank B. Kellogg.

3. In 1928, the Kellogg-Briand Pact called for
   A. an open door to trade in China.
   B. obedience of the League of Nations.
   C. a "good neighbor" policy throughout the world.
   D. the outlawing of war.

4. The "good neighbor" policy applied to
   A. western Europe.
   B. eastern Asia.
   C. Canada and Mexico.
   D. Latin America.

5. An exception to America's insularity in the early 1930s was its
   A. official recognition of the Soviet Union.
   B. military intervention in Japan.
   C. bombing of Shanghai.
   D. support for Franco in the Spanish Civil War.

6. Britain and France finally went to war with Germany after Germany
   A. seized Czechoslovakia.
   B. forced union with Austria.
   C. bombed Munich.
   D. attacked Poland.

7. The term "merchants of death" referred to
   A. Hitler and Mussolini.
   B. business interests that profited from World War I.
   C. the British navy.
   D. isolationists who allowed Hitler to take control of Europe.

8. The Neutrality Act of 1939
   A. required Americans to be neutral in thought as well as in deed.
   B. prevented any assistance to Franco in the Spanish Civil War.
   C. quarantined all nations engaged in anarchy and instability.
   D. allowed the Allies to buy anything for cash and take it away in their own ships.

9. In the 1940 campaign, FDR pledged to
   A. defeat the Axis powers.
   B. stay out of foreign wars.
   C. insure the safety of Britain and France.
   D. defend the Spanish Republicans.

10. The first beneficiaries of lend-lease were
    A. Russia and Germany.
    B. China and Britain.
    C. Japan and France.
    D. France and Britain.

11. The war aims of the Allies were spelled out in the
    A. Kellogg-Briand Pact.
    B. Four Freedoms.
    C. Atlantic Charter.
    D. American declaration of war.

12. The Japanese attack on Pearl Harbor
    A. missed vital shore installations and oil tanks.
    B. sank or severely damaged all U.S. aircraft carriers in the Pacific.
    C. killed 25,000 Americans.
    D. was a complete success.

True-False Questions

Indicate whether each statement is true or false.

1. Under President Harding, the United States eventually did join the League of Nations.
2. The agreements at the Washington Armaments Conference were enforced by the League of Nations.
3. President Hoover never sent the military into Latin America.
4. In the 1930s actual conflict first erupted in Europe.
5. Mussolini rose to power in Italy in the 1920s.
6. In 1935 Italy began to conquer Ethiopia.
7. The Neutrality Act of 1935 prohibited the sale of arms to all belligerents in a war.
8. As extended by Congress in 1937, neutrality laws allowed assistance to either side in the Spanish Civil War.
9. Congress adopted the first peacetime conscription in American history in September 1940.

10. For a third term as president, FDR defeated Wendell Willkie in 1940.
11. The American First Committee was composed of isolationists.
12. The United States declared war on Japan and Germany on December 7, 1941.

Essay Questions

1. What did the United States do in the 1920s to achieve peace and disarmament? Were the efforts successful?
2. How did the United States's relations with Latin America change between 1920 and 1941? Did they improve or not?
3. What actions in the 1930s by Japan, Germany, and Italy did the United States see as aggressive? How did the United States respond?
4. What were the isolationists' arguments in the 1930s? In what ways were they wise or foolish?
5. Was the United States more isolationist in its foreign policy from 1920 to 1929 or from 1930 to 1939? Explain.
6. Why did the United States become involved in World War II? What were the immediate and the more long-term causes?

ANSWERS TO MULTIPLE-CHOICE AND TRUE-FALSE QUESTIONS

Multiple-Choice Questions

1-C, 2-B, 3-D, 4-D, 5-A, 6-D, 7-B, 8-D, 9-B, 10-B, 11-C, 12-A

True-False Questions

1-F, 2-F, 3-T, 4-F, 5-T, 6-T, 7-T, 8-F, 9-T, 10-T, 11-T, 12-F

29 ∽

THE SECOND WORLD WAR

CHAPTER OBJECTIVES

After you complete the reading and study of this chapter, you should be able to

1. Describe the major military strategies in both the European and Pacific Theaters.
2. Explain the problems relating to mobilization and financing of the war.
3. Evaluate the impact of the war on the economy.
4. Assess the impact of the war on women, blacks, Japanese Americans, and the West.
5. Explain the decisions made at the Yalta Conference.
6. Understand the decision to use the atomic bomb and discuss its consequences.

CHAPTER OUTLINE

I. America's early battles
  A. Retreat in the Pacific
    1. Surrender of the Philippines
    2. Japanese strategy
  B. Two naval battles
    1. Coral Sea
    2. Midway: a turning point

II. Mobilization at home
  A. End of depression

B. Economic conversion to war
  1. War Production Board
  2. Role of the Office of Scientific Research and Development
  3. Effects of wartime spending
C. Financing the war
  1. Taxes
  2. National debt
D. Impact of the war on the economy
  1. Labor shortages
  2. Personal incomes
  3. Efforts to control prices
  4. Efforts at conservation
E. Domestic conservatism
  1. Republican gains
  2. Fate of New Deal programs
  3. Effects on organized labor

III. Social effects of the war
  A. Development of the West
    1. Population growth and movement
    2. Defense contracts
    3. Housing shortages
  B. Women in the civilian workforce and the military
  C. Effects of the war on blacks
    1. Problems of the segregated armed forces
    2. March on Washington Movement

3. Challenges to other forms of discrimination
4. White counterreaction
D. Hispanics in the labor force
   1. Recruitment
   2. *Bracero* program
   3. Ethnic tensions
E. Native Americans support war
F. Impact of the war on Japanese Americans
   1. General effect of the war on civil liberties
   2. Internment

IV. The war in Europe
A. War aims and strategy
   1. Europe first
   2. Alliance with Britain
      a. Differences over strategy
      b. War aims
B. North Africa
   1. Defeat of Germans
   2. Casablanca Conference
      a. Attack Sicily and Italy
      b. Unconditional surrender
C. Battle of the Atlantic
D. Sicily and Italy
   1. Invasion of Sicily
   2. Italian surrender
   3. German control of northern Italy
   4. The battle for Rome
E. Strategic bombing of Europe
   1. British and American cooperation
   2. Impact of the bombing
F. Decisions of the Teheran Conference
G. The D-Day invasion
   1. Development and implementation of Operation "Overlord"
   2. German preparations and reaction
   3. Invasion

V. The war in the Pacific
A. Guadalcanal offensive
B. MacArthur's sweep up the western Pacific
   1. Approval for the MacArthur plan
   2. The technique of "leapfrogging"
C. Nimitz's moves in the Central Pacific
D. The naval battle of Leyte Gulf

VI. The end of the war
A. Election of 1944
   1. Republican strategy
   2. Campaign results
B. Converging on Germany
   1. German counteroffensive
   2. Allied moves
   3. Berlin and the Soviets
C. The Yalta Conference
   1. Nature of the decisions
   2. Call for a United Nations
   3. Occupation of Germany
   4. Eastern Europe
   5. Assessment of results
D. Collapse of the Third Reich
   1. FDR's death
   2. V-E Day
   3. Discovery of the Holocaust
E. War in the Pacific
   1. Iwo Jima and Okinawa
   2. Effects of battles
F. The atomic bomb
   1. Manhattan Project
   2. Decision to use the bomb
   3. Use of the bombs
   4. Effects of the bombings
   5. Negotiations for surrender
G. Assessing the war
   1. Death and destruction
   2. Impact on American society

KEY ITEMS OF CHRONOLOGY

March on Washington Movement	1941
Battle of the Coral Sea	May 1942
Battle of Midway	June 1942
Internment of Japanese	1942–1945
Casablanca Conference	January 1943

Abolition of WPA, NYA, CCC	1943
Smith-Connally War Labor Disputes Act	1943
Teheran Conference	November–December 1943
Smith v. *Allwright*	1944
Allies take Rome	June 4, 1944
D-Day	June 6, 1944
General Tojo and his cabinet resign	July 18, 1944
Battle of Leyte Gulf	October 1944
FDR elected to fourth term	November 1944
Battle of the Bulge	December 1944
Yalta Conference	February 1945
Battle of Iwo Jima	February 1945
Battle of Okinawa	April-June 1945
FDR's death—Truman president	April 12, 1945
V-E Day	May 8, 1945
Potsdam Conference	July 1945
Atomic bomb dropped on Hiroshima	August 6, 1945
Japan's surrender	September 2, 1945

TERMS TO MASTER

Listed below are some important terms or people with which you should be familiar after you complete the study of this chapter. Identify or explain each.

1. Battle of Midway
2. General Douglas MacArthur
3. War Production Board
4. Office of Price Administration
5. rationing
6. "right-to-work" laws
7. WACS and WAVES
8. A. Philip Randolph
9. *Smith* v. *Allwright*
10. *bracero* program
11. "Zoot suits"
12. War Relocation Camps
13. Winston Churchill
14. General Dwight D. Eisenhower
15. Vichy government
16. unconditional surrender
17. Operation "Overlord"
18. D-Day
19. "leapfrogging"
20. Battle of Leyte Gulf
21. Harry S. Truman
22. Battle of the Bulge
23. Yalta Conference
24. United Nations
25. Third Reich
26. Battle of Iwo Jima
27. Battle of Okinawa
28. Potsdam Conference

VOCABULARY BUILDING

Listed below are some words used in this chapter. Look in the dictionary for the meaning of each.

1. proximity
2. genocide
3. attribute
4. incalculable
5. tenaciously
6. cryptanalysts
7. allot
8. inflation
9. chafe
10. garner
11. watershed
12. valor
13. animate
14. encode
15. decipher

16. internment
17. succumb
18. affirm
19. pincers
20. interlace
21. array
22. breach
23. impregnable
24. expedite
25. acquiesce
26. temper (v.)
27. pall
28. labyrinth
29. repository
30. circumspect

EXERCISES FOR UNDERSTANDING

When you have completed reading the chapter, answer each of the following questions. If you have difficulty, go back and reread the section of the chapter related to the question.

Multiple-Choice Questions

Select the letter of the response that best completes the statement.

1. The Battle of Midway was the turning point of the war in the Pacific because that battle
   A. stopped the eastward advance of the Japanese.
   B. destroyed most of what was left of the American fleet after Pearl Harbor.
   C. destroyed the Japanese fleet so that they were unable to pursue naval war after this.
   D. placed the United States Air Force close enough to the mainland of Japan to carry out bombing raids there.
2. To finance the war effort, President Roosevelt wanted to rely on
   A. taxes.
   B. borrowing from the public.
   C. loans from the Allies.
   D. reparations from the Germans and Japanese.

3. The basic American economic problem during the war was
   A. stubborn poverty.
   B. shortage of jobs.
   C. runaway inflation.
   D. shortage of workers.
4. After the 1942 congressional elections,
   A. FDR had even larger Democratic majorities in Congress.
   B. Republicans swung to support FDR at home and abroad.
   C. conservatives abolished many New Deal agencies.
   D. Republicans took direction of the war effort.
5. World War II was a watershed for women because they
   A. finally got the right to join labor unions.
   B. joined the labor force in large numbers.
   C. had fewer children than ever before.
   D. gained the right to vote.
6. The most explosive domestic issue ignited by the war involved
   A. rationing of consumer goods.
   B. black employment in the war effort.
   C. right-to-work laws and the formation of unions.
   D. government price controls to prevent inflation.
7. The Supreme Court decision in *Smith* v. *Allwright*
   A. approved the internment of Japanese Americans.
   B. said FDR could run for a fourth term.
   C. outlawed the last of the New Deal programs.
   D. ended whites-only primary elections.
8. Under the *braceros* program
   A. Mexican farm workers came to the United States.
   B. Mexican Americans received free clothing.
   C. Mexico agreed to remain neutral in the war.
   D. the federal government provided housing for Mexican Americans.
9. During World War II, more than 100,000 Americans of Japanese descent
   A. were placed in relocation camps.

B. lost their homes and property.

C. lost most of their civil liberties.

D. all of the above

10. Defeating Hitler was the top priority in World War II because

A. Germany posed the greatest threat to North America.

B. Germany had scientists capable of inventing some awesome weapon.

C. German war potential exceeded Japan's.

D. all of the above

11. D-Day occurred on

A. December 7, 1941.

B. June 6, 1944.

C. April 12, 1945.

D. August 6, 1945.

12. The general in charge of D-Day was

A. George Patton.

B. Douglas MacArthur.

C. Omar Bradley.

D. Dwight Eisenhower.

13. The practice of "leapfrogging" involved

A. moving from island to island in the Pacific after destroying the Japanese army on each island.

B. jumping from North Africa to Sicily to Italy.

C. using naval and air power to neutralize Japanese Pacific island strongholds.

D. a complex convoying system to get supplies across the Atlantic to America's allies.

14. The correct order of events is

A. Potsdam, Yalta, V-E Day, FDR's death.

B. FDR's death, Potsdam, Yalta, V-J Day.

C. FDR's death, V-E Day, Hiroshima, V-J Day.

D. Yalta, FDR's death, V-E Day, Potsdam.

15. The effects of World War II on American society included

A. ending the Great Depression.

B. providing new opportunities for women.

C. developing new technologies that transformed the economy.

D. all of the above

True-False Questions

Indicate whether each statement is true or false.

1. The War Production Board directed the conversion of private industries to war production.

2. The national debt in 1945 was not much larger than it had been in 1941.

3. Inflation was a worse problem in World War II than it had been in World War I.

4. Right-to-work laws assisted the growth of labor unions.

5. During World War II, the fastest growing part of the nation was the urban South.

6. A. Philip Randolph led the March on Washington Movement.

7. "Zoot suit" riots occurred among blacks in Detroit in 1943.

8. The American record on civil liberties during World War II was better than during World War I because so few people opposed the war.

9. The wartime goal of unconditional surrender was designed to reassure Stalin.

10. Allied success in the Atlantic was greatly aided by the invention of radar.

11. Operation "Overlord" was the name given to MacArthur's campaign in the Pacific.

12. The largest naval engagement in history occurred at Leyte Gulf in the Philippines.

13. At the end of the war, the Soviet Union took Berlin because Churchill thought the city was unimportant.

14. One reason that the United States used the atomic bomb was to intimidate Germany and Hitler into surrendering.

15. In proportion to its population, the United States suffered more casualties than any of its allies.

Essay Questions

1. During World War II, how did American military strategy against Germany compare to its strategy against Japan?

2. What were the major social and economic effects of World War II on American society?

3. What were the three or four key battles in World War II? Why was each significant?
4. How did the war affect American minorities?
5. How did decisions reached during the war affect the postwar era?
6. What were the major issues at Yalta and Potsdam? How were they resolved?
7. Why did the United States use the atomic bomb against Japan?

ANSWERS TO MULTIPLE-CHOICE AND TRUE-FALSE QUESTIONS

Multiple-Choice Questions

1-A, 2-A, 3-D, 4-C, 5-B, 6-B, 7-D, 8-A, 9-D, 10-D, 11-B, 12-D, 13-C, 14-C, 15-D

True-False Questions

1-T, 2-F, 3-F, 4-F, 5-F, 6-T, 7-F, 8-T, 9-T, 10-T, 11-F, 12-T, 13-F, 14-F, 15-T

30

THE FAIR DEAL AND CONTAINMENT

CHAPTER OBJECTIVES

After you complete the reading and study of this chapter, you should be able to

1. Analyze the problems of demobilization and conversion to peacetime production.
2. Account for Truman's troubles with Congress and assess the measure of accomplishment that he achieved.
3. Explain the policy of containment and trace its development to 1950.
4. Describe Truman's reelection in 1948.
5. Assess the strength of McCarthyism in the United States.
6. Explain the origins of the Korean War and trace its major developments.

CHAPTER OUTLINE

I. Demobilization under Truman
   A. The Truman style
      1. Truman's background and character
      2. Domestic proposals of 1945
   B. Demobilization
      1. Rapid reduction of armed forces
      2. Escalation of birthrate
      3. Efforts for economic stabilization

C. Attempts to control inflation
      1. Demands for wage increases
      2. A wave of strikes
      3. Truman's response to strikes
      4. Efforts to control prices
      5. The end of controls
D. Partisan conflict
      1. Elections of 1946
      2. Republican Congress
         a. Taft-Hartley Act
         b. Efforts for tax reduction
         c. The National Security Act

II. Development of the cold war
   A. Creating the United Nations
      1. Background of the U.N.
      2. Scheme of its operations
      3. U.S. ratification of U.N. membership
   B. Differences with the Soviets
      1. Historical debate
      2. Problems relating to eastern Europe
      3. Soviet control
      4. Proposals to control atomic energy
   C. Development of the containment policy
      1. Kennan's theory
      2. Problems in Iran, Turkey, and Greece

3. The Truman Doctrine
4. Greek-Turkish Aid
5. The Marshall Plan
6. Division of Germany
   a. Merger of Allied zones
   b. Berlin Blockade
   c. Berlin Airlift
   d. Creation of West and East Germany
7. Development of NATO
8. Establishment of Israel

III. Truman's domestic policies
A. Civil rights
   1. Wartime background
   2. Truman administration
      a. Truman's attitude
      b. Committee on Civil Rights
      c. Segregation in military
   3. Professional baseball
      a. Jackie Robinson
      b. Branch Rickey
B. The 1948 election
   1. Truman's strategy
   2. The Republican position
   3. Democratic battle over civil rights
   4. Creation of the Dixiecrats
   5. Wallace's Progressive party
   6. Nature of the campaign
   7. Election results
   8. Assessment of the results
C. The fate of the Fair Deal

IV. The cold war heats up
A. Point Four Program
B. China's fall to communism
   1. History of the movement in China

2. Assessment of the Communist victory
C. Escalation of rivalry
   1. Soviet atomic bomb
   2. U.S. work on the hydrogen bomb
   3. U.S. decision to maintain peacetime military force
D. The Korean War
   1. Background to the conflict
   2. Responses to the invasion
      a. U.N. action
      b. Truman's decisions
         i. Strengthen NATO
         ii. Aid to French in Indochina
   3. Military developments
      a. Rout of the U.N. forces
      b. Counterattack
      c. The decision to invade the North
      d. Entry of the Chinese Communists
   4. The dismissal of MacArthur
      a. Reasons for the action
      b. Reactions to the firing
   5. Negotiations for peace
E. Another Red Scare
   1. HUAC
   2. The Alger Hiss case
   3. Conviction of spies
   4. McCarthy's witch-hunt
      a. The emergence of Senator McCarthy
      b. Assessment of his tactics
   5. McCarran Internal Security Act
F. Assessing the cold war

KEY ITEMS OF CHRONOLOGY

Servicemen's Readjustment Act	1944
FDR died	April 1945
Taft-Hartley Act	1947
Truman Doctrine	1947
Marshall Plan launched	1947
HUAC investigates Hollywood	1947
National Security Act	1947
Jackie Robinson integrated major league baseball	April 1947

Berlin Blockade and Berlin Airlift	June 1948–May 1949
Truman ordered end to racial segregation in the military	July 1948
Creation of Israel	1948
Hiss case	1948–1950
Establishment of NATO	April 1949
China became Communist	1949
Senator Joseph McCarthy's speech in Wheeling, West Virginia, citing Communists in the State Department	February 1950
Korean War	June 1950–July 1953
MacArthur dismissed	April 1951

TERMS TO MASTER

Listed below are some important terms or people with which you should be familiar after you complete the study of this chapter. Identify or explain each.

1. baby-boom generation
2. G. I. Bill of Rights
3. Henry A. Wallace
4. union shop
5. Taft-Hartley Act
6. National Security Act, 1947
7. United Nations
8. George F. Kennan
9. containment
10. Truman Doctrine
11. cold war
12. Marshall Plan
13. Berlin Blockade
14. NATO
15. Jackie Robinson
16. Dixiecrats
17. Fair Deal
18. Douglas MacArthur
19. HUAC
20. Alger Hiss
21. Joseph R. McCarthy
22. McCarran Act

VOCABULARY BUILDING

Listed below are some words used in this chapter. Look in the dictionary for the meaning of each.

1. polarize
2. unrelenting
3. anticolonial
4. feisty
5. raucous
6. cohort
7. partisan
8. featherbedding
9. culprits
10. compliant
11. vile
12. brandish
13. basin
14. intermittent
15. graphically
16. virulent
17. drove (n.)
18. laudatory
19. drone
20. futility
21. undaunted
22. castigate
23. pundit
24. plague (v.)
25. intractable
26. tyrannical
27. aversion
28. ploy
29. synchronize
30. relinquish

EXERCISES FOR UNDERSTANDING

When you have completed reading the chapter, answer each of the following questions. If you have difficulty, go back and reread the section of the chapter related to the question.

Multiple-Choice Questions

Select the letter of the response that best completes the statement.

1. Before his election as vice president, Harry Truman had
   A. served as governor of Missouri.
   B. been a United States senator.
   C. never held public office.
   D. only been a cabinet member.

2. In September 1945, immediately after the end of World War II, Truman sent to Congress
   A. his ideas for a Fair Deal for the American people.
   B. a suggestion for nuclear disarmament.
   C. a comprehensive domestic program to enlarge the New Deal.
   D. his proposal for a Marshall Plan to rebuild western Europe.

3. Postwar demobilization was eased by
   A. pent-up demand for consumer goods.
   B. Truman's personal popularity.
   C. permanent wage and price controls.
   D. the Taft-Hartley Act.

4. The Taft-Hartley Act contributed to the
   A. dramatic growth of the CIO.
   B. success of "Operation Dixie."
   C. repeal of the Wagner Act.
   D. enactment of state right-to-work laws.

5. In foreign policy in the late 1940s, Democrats and Republicans
   A. were divided over development of nuclear weapons.
   B. generally cooperated.
   C. disagreed about the merits of the Marshall Plan.
   D. fought over the Berlin airlift.

6. As early as the spring of 1945, trouble with the Soviet Union developed over
   A. governments in eastern Europe.
   B. access to Berlin.

C. the reconstruction of western Europe.
   D. Truman's policy in northern Africa.

7. Originally, containment reflected a concern that the Soviets
   A. had nuclear weapons.
   B. sought to control more that just eastern Europe.
   C. would soon invade western Europe and the Middle East.
   D. planned to attack the United States.

8. Truman's aid program to rescue western Europe was called
   A. containment.
   B. the Truman Doctrine.
   C. Point Four.
   D. the Marshall Plan.

9. In the 1948 election, Truman's strategy erred in
   A. underestimating the Dixiecrat rebellion.
   B. overestimating his appeal to black voters.
   C. calling a special session of Congress.
   D. engaging in televised debates with Dewey.

10. The Dixiecrat candidate for president was
    A. Henry Wallace.
    B. Dwight Eisenhower.
    C. George Wallace.
    D. Strom Thurmond.

11. The Democratic Congress reacted to Truman's Fair Deal proposals by
    A. repealing Taft-Hartley.
    B. enacting most of his major proposals.
    C. rejecting federal aid to education and national health insurance.
    D. all of the above

12. A major departure in United States defense policy in 1950 was
    A. joining the North Atlantic Treaty Organization.
    B. rebuilding conventional military forces in peacetime.
    C. moving ahead with the construction of a hydrogen bomb.
    D. sending troops abroad to Korea.

13. "Communism has passed beyond the use of subversion to conquer independent nations and will now use armed invasion and war," said Truman about
    A. Poland.

B. Greece and Turkey.
C. Korea.
D. Berlin.
14. General MacArthur's daring decision in the Korean War was to invade at
A. Seoul.
B. Inchon.
C. Panmunjom.
D. the China border.
15. Communists were required to register with the attorney-general under the
A. Truman Doctrine.
B. executive order issued by Truman.
C. Taft-Hartley Act.
D. McCarran Internal Security Act.

8. Soon after the Berlin Airlift, Germany was divided into two separate nations.
9. Israel was formed in 1948.
10. In 1948, Truman ordered an end to racial segregation in federal employment.
11. Harry Truman won the 1948 election with a minority of the popular vote.
12. Fourteen other members of the United Nations sent troops to fight in Korea.
13. The major issue in Truman's removal of MacArthur was winning the war.
14. Alger Hiss was convicted of espionage.
15. Joseph McCarthy was a Republican senator from Wisconsin.

True-False Questions

Indicate whether each statement is true or false.

1. The G.I. Bill of Rights protected soldiers taken prisoner during the Korean War.
2. The most acute economic problem facing Truman was unemployment.
3. As a result of the 1946 elections, the Republicans gained control of Congress for the first time since the Coolidge administration.
4. In a "closed shop," union workers could not be hired.
5. The Central Intelligence Agency was created by the National Security Act of 1947.
6. The Truman Doctrine grew out of assistance to rebuild Japan.
7. The United States shared control of East Berlin with France and Great Britain.

Essay Questions

1. What were the problems involved in demobilization and reconversion? Did the Truman administration solve them?
2. Harry Truman has often been rated a great president. Do you agree? Why or why not?
3. What was the policy of containment? What were its origins and its effects?
4. Why was the election of 1948 such a surprise? How did Truman manage to pull the upset?
5. The civil rights movement is usually seen as a phenomenon of the 1950s and 1960s. What happened in the area of civil rights during the 1940s?
6. How and why did the Korean War begin?
7. Why did Truman fire MacArthur? Was his action justified? What reactions did it bring?
8. What was the Second Red Scare all about? Was it necessary? What did it accomplish?

ANSWERS TO MULTIPLE-CHOICE AND TRUE-FALSE QUESTIONS

Multiple-Choice Questions

1-B, 2-C, 3-A, 4-D, 5-B, 6-A, 7-B, 8-D, 9-A, 10-D, 11-C, 12-B, 13-C, 14-B, 15-D

True-False Questions

1-F, 2-F, 3-T, 4-F, 5-T, 6-F, 7-F, 8-T, 9-T, 10-T, 11-T, 12-T, 13-F, 14-F, 15-T

31

THROUGH THE PICTURE WINDOW:
SOCIETY AND CULTURE, 1945–1960

CHAPTER OBJECTIVES

After you complete the reading and study of this chapter, you should be able to

1. Account for the emergence of a consumer culture in the prosperous postwar era.
2. Describe the growth of suburban America after World War II.
3. Illustrate the widespread conformity in American culture in the 1950s.
4. Describe the youth culture of the 1950s.
5. Understand the ideas of the major critics of conformity.
6. Explain the artistic and literary dissent beginning in the l950s.

CHAPTER OUTLINE

I. Postwar economy
  A. Growth and prosperity
    1. Military spending
    2. International trade dominance
    3. Technological innovation
    4. Consumer demand
    5. GI Bill of Rights
      a. Provisions
      b. Limitations for blacks

    6. "Baby boom"
  B. Consumer culture
    1. Home ownership
    2. Limited involvement for blacks
    3. Advertising
    4. Credit cards
    5. Shopping malls
  C. Growth of suburbs
    1. Rural-to-urban migration
    2. Levittowns
    3. Automobiles and roads
    4. "White flight"
  D. Great black migration
    1. Southern sources
    2. Urban North and Midwest

II. Postwar conformity
  A. Women and cult of domesticity
    1. Middle-class ideal
    2. "Back to the kitchen"
  B. Search for community
    1. Mobility
    2. Joining organizations
    3. Church growth
      a. Religious revival
      b. Reassurance
      c. Norman Vincent Peale's "positive thinking"

III. Challenges to complacency
  A. Intellectual critics
    1. Reinhold Niebuhr
    2. John Kenneth Galbraith's *Affluent Society*
    3. John Keats's *Crack in the Picture Window*
    4. David Riesman and *The Lonely Crowd*
  B. Youth Culture
    1. Influence of Dr. Benjamin Spock
    2. "Teen" subculture
    3. Juvenile delinquency
  C. Rock 'n' roll
    1. Bridge between black and white music
    2. Elvis Presley
    3. Controversy
  D. Alienation in the arts
    1. Drama
      a. Sense of alienation
      b. Arthur Miller's *Death of a Salesman*

  2. The novel
    a. The individual's struggle for meaning
    b. J. D. Salinger's *Catcher in the Rye*
    c. Saul Bellow, Ralph Ellison, Joseph Heller, Norman Mailer, Joyce Carol Oates, et al.
  3. Painting
    a. Edward Hopper and desolate loneliness
    b. Abstract expressionism
      i. Jackson Pollock
      ii. William de Kooning, Mark Rothko, et al.
  4. The Beats
    a. Liberation of self-expression
    b. Greenwich Village background
    c. William Burroughs, Allen Ginsberg, and Jack Kerouac
    d. Influences

KEY ITEMS OF CHRONOLOGY

Dr. Benjamin Spock, *Common Sense Book of Baby and Child Care*	1946
The first Levittown in New York	1947
Arthur Miller, *Death of a Salesman*	1949
David Riesman, *The Lonely Crowd*	1950
J. D. Salinger, *The Catcher in the Rye*	1951
Ralph Ellison, *Invisible Man*	1952
Allen Ginsburg, *Howl*	1956
Jack Kerouac, *On the Road*	1967
John Kenneth Galbraith, *The Affluent Society*	1958
Vance Packard, *The Waste Makers*	1960

TERMS TO MASTER

Listed below are some important terms or people with which you should be familiar after you complete the study of this chapter. Identify or explain each.

1. GI Bill
2. baby-boom generation
3. suburbs
4. William Levitt
5. "white flight"
6. white collar
7. cult of domesticity
8. Norman Vincent Peale
9. Reinhold Niebuhr
10. "other directed"

11. Benjamin Spock
12. "Silent generation"
13. juvenile delinquency
14. rock 'n' roll
15. Alan Freed
16. Elvis Presley
17. *Death of a Salesman*
18. J. D. Salinger
19. abstract expressionism
20. Jackson Pollock
21. The Beats
22. Jack Kerouac
23. *Howl*

VOCABULARY BUILDING

Listed below are some words used in this chapter. Look in the dictionary for the meaning of each.

1. deprivation
2. chasm
3. giddy
4. catapult
5. catalyst
6. dismantle
7. prolific
8. dispersion
9. gloss
10. corrosive
11. corridor
12. proliferation
13. dysfunctional
14. enclave
15. veritable
16. chronic
17. gangrene
18. regimentation
19. gregarious
20. cavort
21. larceny
22. pagan
23. manifest (v.)
24. melancholy
25. aesthetic
26. vibrant
27. mundane
28. bohemian

29. affinity
30. existential

EXERCISES FOR UNDERSTANDING

When you have completed reading the chapter, answer each of the following questions. If you have difficulty, go back and reread the section of the chapter related to the question.

Multiple-Choice Questions

Select the letter of the response that best completes the statement.

1. The major catalyst for economic growth after 1945 was
   A. government spending.
   B. international trade.
   C. pent-up consumer demand.
   D. the cold war.
2. The "baby boom" peaked in
   A. 1946.
   B. 1957.
   C. 1964.
   D. 1973.
3. The leader of the suburban revolution was
   A. Norman Vincent Peale.
   B. J. D. Salinger.
   C. Alan Freed.
   D. William Levitt.
4. As a result of the great migration of southern blacks, the largest concentration of African Americans is in
   A. the South Side of Chicago.
   B. Harlem in New York City.
   C. the Watts section of Los Angeles.
   D. Washington, D.C.
5. During the 1950s, the percentage of women working outside the home
   A. declined by half.
   B. finally equaled the rate for men.
   C. increased.
   D. stayed the same.
6. The leading promoter of a feel-good theology as found in *The Power of Positive Thinking* was
   A. Reinhold Niebuhr.

B. Norman Vincent Peale.
C. Billy Graham.
D. David Riesman.
7. Critics of conformity and complacency included
   A. William Levitt and Reinhold Niebuhr.
   B. J. Edgar Hoover and Willy Loman.
   C. Norman Vincent Peale and Tennessee Williams.
   D. David Riesman and Allen Ginsburg.
8. David Riesman pioneered the concept of
   A. the affluent society.
   B. juvenile delinquency.
   C. the other-directed personality.
   D. a postwar "baby-boom" generation.
9. Rock 'n' roll music was directly related to
   A. abstract expressionism.
   B. rhythm and blues.
   C. neo-orthodoxy.
   D. the Beat generation.
10. Arthur Miller's *Death of a Salesman* portrayed the theme of
    A. alienation in a mass culture.
    B. the benefits of an affluent society.
    C. belongingness in suburban America.
    D. the religious promise of neo-orthodoxy.
11. An exploration of a young man's search for meaning was
    A. *Rabbit, Run.*
    B. *The Robe.*
    C. *The Catcher in the Rye.*
    D. *The Grapes of Wrath.*
12. The Beats included
    A. Arthur Miller, Edward Albee, and Tennessee Williams.
    B. Willem de Kooning, Mark Rothko, and Robert Motherwell.
    C. William Burroughs, Allen Ginsberg, and Jack Kerouac.
    D. none of the above

True-False Questions

Indicate whether each statement is true or false.

1. The GI Bill helped veterans further their education.
2. The gap between the average yearly incomes of blacks and whites narrowed during the 1950s.
3. In the early 1960s, 20 percent of Americans lived between Boston and Norfolk, Virginia.
4. The federal government helped spur the growth of suburbs by insuring home loans for a larger percentage of the cost of homes.
5. The migration of southern blacks after World War II was not as large as the migration after World War I.
6. The postwar era of alienation resulted in a decline in church membership.
7. The leader of the neo-orthodox religious movement was Reinhold Niebuhr.
8. John Keats's *The Crack in the Picture Window* was a critique of juvenile delinquency.
9. Alan Freed was a major early performer of rock 'n' roll music.
10. Elvis Presley was a white male from Detroit.
11. The leading abstract expressionist painter was Jackson Pollock.
12. The origin of the Beats was Greenwich Village in New York City.

Essay Questions

1. What effects did economic prosperity have on society in the 1950s?
2. How relevant are the concepts of consensus, conformity, and consumerism to black life in the 1950s?
3. How did the ideas and values of Norman Vincent Peale and William Levitt differ from those of Arthur Miller and Jackson Pollock?
4. What was the youth culture of the 1950s and how did it differ from the larger adult culture?
5. What might the Beats have said about rock 'n' roll?
6. How would Jack Kerouac and Willy Loman respond to Levittown? Explain.

ANSWERS TO MULTIPLE-CHOICE AND TRUE-FALSE QUESTIONS

Multiple-Choice Questions

1-C, 2-B, 3-D, 4-A, 5-C, 6-B, 7-D, 8-C, 9-B, 10-A, 11-C, 12-C

True-False Questions

1-T, 2-F, 3-T, 4-T, 5-F, 6-F, 7-T, 8-F, 9-F, 10-F, 11-T, 12-T

32 ∞

CONFLICT AND DEADLOCK:
THE EISENHOWER YEARS

CHAPTER OBJECTIVES

After you complete the reading and study of this chapter, you should be able to

1. Describe Eisenhower's style and his approach to the nation's problems.
2. Assess the nature of modern Republicanism in relation to New Deal liberalism, focusing especially on Eisenhower's stance on key domestic legislation.
3. Assess the early performance of Dulles's diplomacy, especially as compared to the policy of containment.
4. Explain the origins of the Indochina War and assess Eisenhower's response to it.
5. Explain the Suez Crisis and the Hungarian revolt, their interrelations and their consequences.
6. Evaluate the impact of Sputnik.
7. Describe the developments in civil rights in the Eisenhower era and assess his responses to them.

CHAPTER OUTLINE

   I. Election of 1952
      A. Appeal of Ike
      B. Adlai Stevenson
      C. Results

  II. The early Eisenhower administration
      A. Ike's background
      B. Appointments
      C. Dynamic conservatism
         1. Some New Deal programs cut
           a. Reconstruction Finance Corporation
           b. Wage and price controls
         2. Some New Deal programs extended
           a. Social Security
           b. Minimum wage
           c. Health care
           d. Housing
      D. Public works
         1. St. Lawrence Seaway
         2. Interstate highways
      E. Armistice in Korea
         1. Ike's bold stand
         2. Reasons for settlement
      F. End to McCarthyism
         1. McCarthy's tactics
         2. McCarthy and the army
         3. Senate condemnation
      G. Internal security worries

 III. Foreign policy in the first term
      A. Dulles and foreign policy
         1. Dulles's background
         2. Idea of liberation
         3. Covert action

4. Massive retaliation
5. Brinksmanship
B. Problems in Indochina
  1. Background to war
    a. Nationalism in Asia
    b. French control
    c. Ho Chi Minh and independence
  2. First Indochina War
    a. Outbreak of fighting
    b. American aid
    c. Geneva Accords
  3. Creation of SEATO
  4. Government of Diem
    a. Need for reform
    b. Opposition suppressed

IV. Foreign crises in the second administration
A. Election of 1956
  1. Eisenhower's health
  2. Stevenson defeated again
B. The Suez crisis
  1. Eisenhower's Middle East policy
  2. Rise of Nasser in Egypt
  3. Offer and withdrawal of loan
  4. Nasser's seizure of Suez
  5. Israeli invasion
  6. Resolution of crisis
C. The Hungarian revolt
  1. De-Stalinization
  2. Hungarian revolt
  3. Soviet repression
D. Sputnik
  1. The Soviet feat
  2. American reactions
    a. U.S. space effort
    b. Deployment of missiles

c. Creation of NASA
d. National Defense Education Act
E. Persisting problems
  1. Middle East
    a. Eisenhower Doctrine
    b. Troops to Lebanon
  2. Soviet pressure on Berlin
  3. U-2 Summit
  4. Cuba
    a. Castro's takeover
    b. American responses

V. The early civil rights movement
A. Eisenhower's views of civil rights
B. Court decisions
  1. Decisions preliminary to *Brown*
  2. The *Brown* decision
  3. Reactions to *Brown*
    a. Ike's reluctance
    b. Token compliance
    c. Massive resistance
      i. Citizens' Councils
      ii. Southern Manifesto
C. Montgomery bus boycott
  1. Causes for action
  2. Role of Martin Luther King, Jr.
  3. Results
D. Civil rights legislation
E. Little Rock
  1. Court order
  2. Governor Faubus
  3. Federal intervention

VI. Assessing the Eisenhower years
A. Accomplishments
B. Farewell address

KEY ITEMS OF CHRONOLOGY

Twenty-second Amendment ratified	1951
Eisenhower elected president	1952
Fall of Dien Bien Phu	May 1954
Brown v. *Board of Education*	May 1954
Geneva Accords signed	July 1954
SEATO created	September 1954
McCarthy condemned by the Senate	December 1954
Montgomery bus boycott	December 1955–December 1956

Suez crisis (and Hungarian revolt)	October 1956
Little Rock High School crisis	September 1957
Sputnik launched	October 1957
U-2 incident	May 1960

TERMS TO MASTER

Listed below are some important terms or people with which you should be familiar after you complete the study of this chapter. Identify or explain each.

1. Twenty-second Amendment
2. Adlai Stevenson
3. "hidden-hand" presidency
4. "dynamic conservatism"
5. St. Lawrence Seaway
6. interstate highway system
7. John Foster Dulles
8. Joseph R. McCarthy
9. Army-McCarthy hearings
10. Earl Warren
11. "liberation"
12. "massive retaliation"
13. brinksmanship
14. Indochina
15. Ho Chi Minh
16. Dien Bien Phu
17. Geneva Accords
18. SEATO
19. Nikita Khrushchev
20. Suez crisis
21. Sputnik
22. NASA
23. Eisenhower Doctrine
24. U-2 incident
25. *Brown* v. *Board of Education*
26. Citizens' Councils
27. Martin Luther King, Jr.
28. Montgomery bus boycott

4. novice
5. dissimulation
6. passivity
7. hobnob
8. renege
9. meteoric
10. blackmail
11. sully
12. edict
13. tactician
14. meshed
15. deplore
16. covert
17. deterrence
18. brink
19. obliged
20. bulwark
21. superficial
22. quandary
23. satellite
24. acronym
25. syndrome
26. compound
27. joust
28. prerequisite
29. interpose
30. contiguous

EXERCISES FOR UNDERSTANDING

When you have completed reading the chapter, answer each of the following questions. If you have difficulty, go back and reread the section of the chapter related to the question.

VOCABULARY BUILDING

Listed below are some words used in this chapter. Look in the dictionary for the meaning of each.

1. formidable
2. incumbent
3. harass

Multiple-Choice Questions

Select the letter of the response that best completes the statement.

1. In the 1952 campaign, Eisenhower promised to
   A. destroy Joseph McCarthy.
   B. end the Social Security system.

    C. go to Korea.

    D. appoint Adlai Stevenson to his cabinet.

2. The Twenty-second Amendment to the Constitution
   A. ended prohibition.
   B. restricted presidents to two terms.
   C. ended poll taxes in state and local elections.
   D. gave eighteen-year-olds the right to vote.

3. Dynamic conservatism was defined as being
   A. liberal on civil rights but conservative on welfare.
   B. conservative on financial matters but liberal regarding people.
   C. radical on foreign policy but conservative on the budget.
   D. liberal on fiscal policy but conservative on military affairs.

4. Eisenhower said that the "biggest damnfool mistake I ever made" was
   A. picking Richard Nixon as his running mate.
   B. putting Earl Warren on the Supreme Court.
   C. not using the atomic bomb in Korea.
   D. getting the nation involved in the war in Vietnam.

5. The Republican policy of "liberation" was aimed at
   A. African Americans.
   B. European colonies in Africa and Asia.
   C. eastern Europe.
   D. people within the Soviet Union.

6. Massive retaliation and brinksmanship were based on
   A. Democratic opposition to the cold war.
   B. budgetary considerations aimed at saving money.
   C. Eisenhower's background in the air force.
   D. a belief that containment had failed.

7. In Indochina the late 1940s, the United States supported
   A. Japan.
   B. China.
   C. Britain.
   D. France.

8. The United States tried to befriend Egypt in the 1950s by
   A. offering to finance a dam on the Nile River.
   B. cutting ties to Egypt's enemy, Israel.
   C. selling it nuclear weapons.
   D. all of the above

9. In the Suez crisis of 1956, the United States
   A. fought with Israel and Britain.
   B. sent troops to protect the Suez Canal.
   C. sided with the Soviet Union.
   D. stayed completely neutral.

10. Results of the successful launching of Sputnik included
    A. the establishment of NASA.
    B. increased defense spending.
    C. more federal aid to education.
    D. all of the above

11. In *Brown* v. *Board of Education,* the Supreme Court ruled that
    A. racial segregation was constitutional.
    B. "separate but equal" in public education was unconstitutional.
    C. all children under the age of eighteen had to attend school.
    D. Kansas must provide free education for Indian children.

12. In regard to civil rights, President Eisenhower
    A. desegregated public services in Washington, D.C.
    B. preferred state and local action to federal action.
    C. thought laws could not change racial attitudes.
    D. all of the above

13. Martin Luther King, Jr., was the leader of the
    A. National Association for the Advancement of Colored People.
    B. effort to integrate Little Rock schools.
    C. Montgomery bus boycott.
    D. Citizens' Councils.

14. The Civil Rights Act of 1957 emphasized
    A. voting rights.
    B. school integration.
    C. integration of restaurants, hotels, and theaters.
    D. lynching and mob violence.

15. Eisenhower responded to the Little Rock crisis by
    A. sending army troops to Little Rock.
    B. going to Little Rock personally.
    C. having Governor Faubus arrested.
    D. telling the black students to drop their demands.

True-False Questions

Indicate whether each statement is true or false.

1. Before becoming president, Eisenhower had been a university president.
2. President Eisenhower fought to eliminate many New Deal programs.
3. Major monuments to Eisenhower's presidency include the interstate highway system.
4. Eisenhower threatened to use atomic weapons during the Korean conflict.
5. The United States senate expelled Joseph McCarthy.
6. John Foster Dulles was secretary of defense under Eisenhower.
7. The communist leader in Vietnam was Ho Chi Minh.
8. Dien Bien Phu was a major victory for the United States's ally in Vietnam.
9. To prevent the spread of communism in southeast Asia, the United States established SEATO in 1954.
10. For the first time since Reconstruction, the Republicans won a Deep South state in 1956.
11. The Eisenhower Doctrine applied to southeast Asia.
12. Fidel Castro took power in Cuba in 1959.
13. In the Southern Manifesto, white southern liberals endorsed school desegregation.
14. The Citizens' Councils wanted to maintain white supremacy.
15. After the Montgomery bus boycott, Martin Luther King, Jr., helped form the Southern Christian Leadership Conference.

Essay Questions

1. Does "dynamic conservatism" or "hidden-hand presidency" better describe the Eisenhower administration? Why?
2. What factors contributed to the fall of Senator McCarthy?
3. Did the Eisenhower administration's cold war foreign policy represent continuity with or a change from earlier policies?
4. Were United States actions in the Middle East, Indochina, and Hungary part of a consistent policy? Explain.
5. How did United States involvement in Indochina after World War II begin?
6. What were the key events in the civil rights movement in the 1950s? Why were they significant?

ANSWERS TO MULTIPLE-CHOICE AND TRUE-FALSE QUESTIONS

Multiple-Choice Questions

1-C, 2-B, 3-B, 4-B, 5-C, 6-B, 7-D, 8-A, 9-C, 10-D, 11-B, 12-D, 13-C, 14-A, 15-A

True-False Questions

1-T, 2-F, 3-T, 4-T, 5-F, 6-F, 7-T, 8-F, 9-T, 10-T, 11-F, 12-T, 13-F, 14-T, 15-T

33

NEW FRONTIERS: POLITICS
AND SOCIAL CHANGE IN THE 1960s

CHAPTER OBJECTIVES

After you complete the reading and study of this chapter, you should be able to

1. Describe Kennedy's style and compare it to the styles of his predecessor and his successor.
2. Assess Kennedy's domestic legislative achievements.
3. Assess the Kennedy record in foreign affairs.
4. Describe and account for LBJ's legislative accomplishments.
5. Explain why the Vietnam War became a quagmire for the United States and why LBJ changed his policy there in 1968.
6. Trace the transformation of the civil rights movement into the black power movement.

CHAPTER OUTLINE

I. The New Frontier
  A. The 1960 election
    1. Nixon's experience
    2. Kennedy's background
    3. Campaign
      a. Televised debates
      b. Results
  B. Start of the administration

    1. Appointments
    2. Inaugural address
  C. Legislative achievements
    1. Urban renewal, minimum wage, social security
    2. Alliance for Progress
    3. Peace Corps
    4. Trade Expansion Act
  D. Warren Court
    1. School prayer
    2. Rights of defendants

II. Civil rights movement
  A. Kennedy's attitude
  B. Mass protests
    1. Sit-ins
      a. Greensboro
      b. Formation of SNCC
    2. Freedom rides
    3. Role of music
  C. Federal action
    1. University of Mississippi
    2. King in Birmingham
      a. New strategy
      b. Letter from jail
    3. University of Alabama
  D. March on Washington, D.C.

III. Kennedy and foreign affairs
  A. Early setbacks
    1. Bay of Pigs disaster

2. Vienna Summit
3. Berlin
B. Cuban missile crisis
1. Causes of crisis
2. Kennedy's action
3. Resolution of crisis
4. Aftereffects
C. Vietnam
1. Neutrality for Laos
2. Problems with Diem
3. Kennedy's reluctance to escalate
4. Overthrow of Diem
D. Assassination of President Kennedy
1. Lee Harvey Oswald
2. Warren Commission
3. Continuing controversy

IV. Lyndon Johnson and the Great Society
A. Johnson's personality
B. War on poverty
1. *The Other America*
2. 1964 tax cut
3. Economic Opportunity Act
C. Election in 1964
1. Goldwater—"choice not echo"
2. LBJ appeals to consensus
3. Johnson landslide
D. Landmark legislation
1. Health insurance
2. Aid to education
3. Appalachian redevelopment
4. Housing and urban development
5. Immigration law of 1965
a. End to national quotas
b. Influx from Asia and Latin America
E. Shortcomings of Great Society

V. From civil rights to black power
A. Civil Rights Act of 1964
1. Public accommodations

2. Suits for school desegregation
3. Equal employment
B. King's Nobel Peace Prize
C. Voting rights
1. King's Selma campaign
2. Johnson support
3. Voting Rights Act
D. Urban rioting
1. Watts riots
2. Other cities
E. Toward black power
1. SNCC
a. Rejection of nonviolence
b. Call for separatism
2. Malcolm X
3. Effects of black power

VI. The tragedy of Vietnam
A. Escalation
1. Gulf of Tonkin Resolution
2. Bombing and combat troops in 1965
B. Context for policy
1. Containment theory
2. Not an accident
3. Erosion of support for war
4. Unity of North Vietnamese
C. Turning point of the war
1. Tet Offensive
2. Presidential primaries
3. LBJ decides not to run

VII. The crescendo of the sixties
A. Assassinations in 1968
1. Martin Luther King, Jr.
2. Robert F. Kennedy
B. Election of 1968
1. Chicago and Miami
2. George Wallace
3. Election of Nixon

KEY ITEMS OF CHRONOLOGY

Greensboro sit-in	1960
Kennedy administration	1961–1963
Bay of Pigs invasion	April 1961
Freedom rides	May 1961
"Letter from Birmingham Jail"	1963

Gideon v. *Wainright*	1963
March on Washington	August 1963
Cuban missile crisis	October 1963
Overthrow of Ngo Dinh Diem	November 1963
Kennedy assassination	November 22, 1963
Escobedo v. *Illinois*	1964
Civil Rights Act (public accommodations)	July 1964
Gulf of Tonkin Resolution	August 1964
Voting Rights Act	1965
Watts riot	August 1965
Malcolm X assassinated	1965
Miranda v. *Arizona*	1966
Tet Offensive	January–February 1968
King assassinated	April 1968
Robert Kennedy assassinated	June 1968
Democratic national convention in Chicago	August 1968
Election of Richard Nixon	November 1968

TERMS TO MASTER

Listed below are some important terms or people with which you should be familiar after you complete the study of this chapter. Identify or explain each.

1. New Frontier
2. Peace Corps
3. *Gideon* v. *Wainright*
4. *Escobedo* v. *Illinois*
5. *Miranda* v. *Arizona*
6. Martin Luther King, Jr.
7. SNCC
8. Freedom rides
9. March on Washington
10. Bay of Pigs invasion
11. Berlin Wall
12. Cuban missile crisis
13. Nuclear Test Ban Treaty
14. Ngo Dinh Diem
15. war on poverty
16. Great Society
17. *The Other America*
18. Medicare and Medicaid
19. Barry Goldwater
20. Civil Rights Act of 1964
21. Voting Rights Act of 1965
22. Watts riot
23. black power
24. Malcolm X
25. Gulf of Tonkin Resolution
26. Viet Cong
27. Tet Offensive
28. Eugene McCarthy
29. Robert Kennedy

VOCABULARY BUILDING

Listed below are some words used in this chapter. Look in the dictionary for the meaning of each.

1. turbulence
2. trauma
3. ideology
4. chameleon
5. dispel
6. liability
7. haggard
8. sinister
9. felony
10. interrogate
11. lament (v.)
12. resolve (n.)
13. preclude
14. insurgent
15. gauntlet
16. mystique

17. torrent
18. savage (v.)
19. bellicose
20. renovate
21. languish
22. indigent
23. parochial
24. amendable
25. estranged
26. preponderant
27. hyperbole
28. ostensibly
29. quagmire
30. extricate

EXERCISES FOR UNDERSTANDING

When you have completed reading the chapter, answer each of the following questions. If you have difficulty, go back and reread the section of the chapter related to the question.

Multiple-Choice Questions

Select the letter of the response that best completes the statement.

1. The turning point in the 1960 election was
   A. the Democratic convention in Chicago.
   B. Nixon's agreeing to debate Kennedy on television.
   C. Eisenhower's surprise endorsement of Kennedy.
   D. the botched Bay of Pigs invasion.
2. One of President Kennedy's legislative achievements was
   A. health insurance for the elderly.
   B. the Voting Rights Act.
   C. the Department of Urban Affairs.
   D. the Trade Expansion Act of 1962.
3. In *Gideon* v. *Wainwright,* the Supreme Court ruled
   A. a poor felony defendant had to be provided a lawyer.
   B. the death penalty was unconstitutional.
   C. copies of the Bible could not be left in public buildings.
   D. public schools had to be desegregated by 1964.

4. The first genuine mass movement in African American history was the
   A. freedom rides.
   B. Selma-to-Montgomery march.
   C. March on Washington.
   D. sit-ins.
5. The correct order for events in the civil rights movement is
   A. Montgomery bus boycott, Greensboro sit-ins, freedom rides, and black power.
   B. freedom rides, Greensboro sit-ins, assassination of King, and Voting Rights Act.
   C. Greensboro sit-ins, Montgomery bus boycott, assassination of Malcolm X, and freedom rides.
   D. Montgomery bus boycott, black power, Voting Rights Act, and Greensboro sit-ins.
6. In the Cuban missile crisis, President Kennedy ordered
   A. surgical air strikes of Cuba.
   B. a quarantine of Cuba.
   C. the Bay of Pigs invasion.
   D. removal of U.S. missiles from Turkey.
7. By the end of 1963, the United States had sent to Vietnam
   A. only 2,000 military advisers.
   B. more than 15,000 military advisers.
   C. 25,000 fighting troops.
   D. over 100,000 fighting troops.
8. The war on poverty was partly inspired by
   A. *The Affluent Society.*
   B. *Invisible Man.*
   C. *The Other America.*
   D. *An American Dilemma.*
9. "I would remind you that extremism in the defense of liberty is no vice," said
   A. Lyndon Johnson.
   B. Earl Warren.
   C. Barry Goldwater.
   D. Richard Nixon.
10. Achievements of the Great Society included
    A. medicare and medicaid.
    B. federal aid to education.
    C. the Department of Housing and Urban Development.
    D. all of the above

11. The most articulate spokesman for black power was
    A. Stokely Carmichael.
    B. Huey Newton.
    C. Martin Luther King, Jr.
    D. Malcolm X.
12. The president received authority to do whatever was necessary in Vietnam under the
    A. Constitution's war-making clause.
    B. War Powers Act of 1964.
    C. Tonkin Gulf Resolution.
    D. Twenty-fourth Amendment to the Constitution.
13. Vietnam was called the "living room war" because
    A. it was so hotly debated in homes across the nation.
    B. so many sons and fathers were in Vietnam.
    C. television brought it into everyone's living room.
    D. service in Vietnam for most soldiers had all the comforts of home.
14. In the Tet Offensive of 1968,
    A. North Vietnamese and Viet Cong attacked all over South Vietnam.
    B. the Americans and South Vietnamese won a counterattack.
    C. the American public suffered a serious psychological blow.
    D. all of the above
15. The correct order of events in 1968 is
    A. Robert Kennedy's death, the assassination of Martin Luther King, Jr., Johnson's declaration he would not seek reelection, and the Chicago convention.
    B. Johnson's declaration he would not seek reelection, Robert Kennedy's death, the Chicago convention, and the assassination of Martin Luther King, Jr.
    C. Johnson's declaration he would not seek reelection, the assassination of Martin Luther King, Jr., Robert Kennedy's death, and the Chicago convention.
    D. the assassination of Martin Luther King, Jr., Johnson's declaration he would not seek reelection, Robert Kennedy's death, and the Chicago convention.

True-False Questions

Indicate whether each statement is true or false.

1. John Kennedy was the youngest person ever elected president.
2. Kennedy's secretary of state was his brother Robert.
3. Kennedy's program for Latin America was called the Alliance for Progress.
4. The freedom riders traveled by bus.
5. Martin Luther King, Jr., delivered his "I Have a Dream" speech in Birmingham.
6. The Bay of Pigs invasion occurred before the Cuban missile crisis.
7. Johnson announced the war on poverty after he called for building the Great Society.
8. In 1964 Johnson defeated Goldwater.
9. The Immigration Act of 1965 ended national quotas.
10. The Civil Rights Act of 1964 barred discrimination by sex in employment.
11. From its beginning in 1960, SNCC disagreed with the idea of nonviolence.
12. The black power movement pushed the civil rights movement to consider poor inner-city blacks.
13. The black power movement encouraged blacks to take pride in their African ancestry and in their accomplishments.
14. By 1966, the United States had only 100,000 soldiers in Vietnam.
15. Richard Nixon was elected in 1968 by a landslide.

Essay Questions

1. Was Kennedy more successful in domestic affairs or foreign policy? Explain.
2. What were the major achievements of the Great Society program? Which were the two or three most important ones?
3. How did United States policy toward Vietnam evolve from 1961 to 1968? What were the turning points?
4. What were the major achievements of the civil rights movement between 1960 and 1968?

5. What was black power, what was its origin, and what effect did it have?
6. Was Lyndon Johnson a great president? Explain.

7. What factors contributed to the election of Richard Nixon in 1968?

ANSWERS TO MULTIPLE-CHOICE AND TRUE-FALSE QUESTIONS

Multiple-Choice Questions

1-B, 2-D, 3-A, 4-D, 5-A, 6-B, 7-B, 8-C, 9-C, 10-D, 11-D, 12-C, 13-C, 14-D, 15-C

True-False Questions

1-T, 2-F, 3-T, 4-T, 5-F, 6-T, 7-F, 8-T, 9-T, 10-T, 11-F, 12-T, 13-T, 14-F, 15-F

34

REBELLION AND REACTION
IN THE 1960s AND 1970s

CHAPTER OBJECTIVES

After you complete the reading and study of this chapter, you should be able to

1. Account for the rise and decline of New Left protests.
2. Describe the counterculture and its impact.
3. Trace the reform movements for women, Hispanics, Indians, and gays.
4. Explain Nixon's aims in Vietnam.
5. Assess the impact of the Vietnam War on American society, military morale, and later foreign policy.
6. Explain Nixon's goals in domestic policy and account for his limited accomplishments.
7. Explain the problems plaguing the United States economy in the 1970s, and describe the various cures Nixon tried.
8. Describe Nixon's foreign policy triumphs in China and the Soviet Union, and explain their significance.
9. Discuss the Watergate cover-up and account for the difficulty in unraveling it.
10. Describe the brief presidency of Gerald Ford.
11. Assess the Carter administration's successes and failures.

CHAPTER OUTLINE

I. Roots of rebellion
  A. Youth revolt
    1. Baby-boomers as young adults
    2. Sit-ins and end of apathy
  B. New Left
    1. Students for a Democratic Society
      a. Port Huron Statement
      b. Participatory democracy
    2. Berkeley Free Speech movement
    3. Antiwar protests
    4. 1968
      a. Columbia University uprising
      b. Democratic convention in Chicago
  C. Counterculture
    1. Descendants of the Beats
    2. Alienated and disillusioned
    3. Rock music
      a. Woodstock
      b. Altamont
  D. Feminism
    1. Betty Friedan's *The Feminine Mystique*
    2. National Organization for Women
    3. Federal actions
      a. Affirmative action
      b. *Roe* v. *Wade*

     c. Equal Rights Amendment's
       failure
    4. Divisions and reactions
  E. Minorities
    1. Hispanic rights
     a. Activism in 1950s and 1960s
     b. United Farm Workers
      i. César Chavez
      ii. Migrant workers
      iii. Grape strike and boycott
     c. Growth of population
    2. American Indians
     a. Emergence of Indian rights
     b. American Indian Movement
     c. Legal actions
    3. Gay rights
     a. Stonewall Inn raid
     b. Gay Liberation Front
     c. Gay rights movement

II. Nixon and Vietnam
  A. Policy of gradual withdrawal
  B. Movement on three fronts
    1. Insistence on Communist
      withdrawal from South Vietnam
    2. Efforts to undercut unrest in the
      United States
    3. Expanded air war
  C. Occasions for public outcry against
    the war
    1. My Lai massacre
    2. Cambodian "incursion"
    3. *Pentagon Papers*
  D. American withdrawal
    1. Kissinger's efforts before the
      1972 election
    2. Christmas bombings
    3. Final acceptance of peace
    4. U.S. withdrawal in March 1973
  E. Ultimate victory of the North:
    March–April 1975
  F. Assessment of the war
    1. Failure to transfer democracy
    2. Erosion of respect for the military
    3. Division of the American people
    4. Cost in lives and money

III. Nixon and Middle America
  A. A reflection of Middle American
    values
  B. Domestic affairs

    1. Civil rights
     a. Nixon opposition
     b. Congress extends Voting
       Rights Act over veto
     c. Court actions
      i. For Mississippi integration
      ii. Support for busing
      iii. Limits on busing
      iv. Restrictions on quotas
      v. Growing conservatism
    2. Twenty-sixth Amendment
    3. Environmental Action
  C. Economic malaise
    1. Causes of stagflation
     a. Spending without taxes
     b. International competition
     c. Energy dependence
     d. Other factors
      i. Oil price rises
      ii. Growing workforce
    2. Nixon's efforts to improve the
      economy
     a. Reducing the federal deficit
     b. Reducing the money supply
     c. Wage and price controls

IV. Nixon's triumphs
  A. Rapprochement with China
  B. Détente with the Soviet Union
    1. The visit to Moscow
    2. The SALT agreement
  C. Kissinger's shuttle diplomacy in the
    Middle East
  D. Election of 1972
    1. Removal of the Wallace threat
    2. The McGovern candidacy
    3. Results of the election

V. Watergate
  A. Unraveling the cover-up
    1. Nixon's personal role
    2. April resignations
    3. The Nixon tapes
    4. The Saturday Night Massacre
    5. The Court decides against the
      president
    6. Articles of impeachment
    7. The resignation
  B. The aftermath of Watergate
    1. Ford's selection

2. The Nixon pardon
3. Resiliency of American institutions
4. War Powers Act
5. Campaign financing legislation
6. Freedom of Information Act

VI. An unelected president
   A. Ford administration
      1. Drift at the end of Nixon administration
      2. Use of veto
      3. Battle with the economy
      4. Diplomatic accomplishments
      5. Loss of South Vietnam
   B. Election of 1976
      1. Ford's nomination
      2. Rise of Jimmy Carter
      3. Carter's victory

VII. Carter presidency
   A. Early domestic moves
      1. Appointments
      2. Amnesty for draft dodgers
      3. Environmental legislation
      4. Energy crisis
      5. Crisis of confidence
   B. Foreign policy initiatives
      1. Human rights
      2. Panama Canal treaties
      3. Camp David Agreement
   C. Troubles
      1. Stagflation
      2. SALT II Treaty
      3. Soviet invasion of Afghanistan
   D. Iranian crisis
      1. Background
      2. Efforts to aid the hostages
      3. End of 444-day crisis

KEY ITEMS OF CHRONOLOGY

Students for a Democratic Society formed	1960
Port Huron Statement	1962
Betty Friedan's *The Feminine Mystique*	1963
Berkeley Free Speech Movement	1964
NOW founded	1966
My Lai massacre	1968
Columbia University demonstrations	1968
Stonewall Inn riot	1969
Americans walked on the moon	July 1969
Woodstock music festival	1969
Cambodian "incursion"	April 1970
Twenty-sixth Amendment	1971
Swann v. *Charlotte-Mecklenburg Board of Education*	1971
Pentagon Papers published	June 1971
Roe v. *Wade*	1972
Nixon's visit to China	February 1972
SALT agreement signed	May 1972
Watergate break-in occurs	June 1972
Nixon reelected	November 1972
Last American troops leave Vietnam	March 1973
War Powers Act	1973
Nixon's resignation	August 9, 1974
South Vietnam falls to the North	April 1975
Jimmy Carter elected president	1976
Bakke v. *Board of Regents of California*	1978

TERMS TO MASTER

Listed below are some important terms or people with which you should be familiar after you complete the study of this chapter. Identify or explain each.

1. New Left
2. SDS
3. participatory democracy
4. Free Speech movement
5. Yippies and hippies
6. counterculture
7. Woodstock
8. Betty Friedan
9. NOW
10. Equal Rights Amendment
11. Chicano
12. César Chavez
13. Stonewall riot
14. My Lai
15. Kent State
16. Henry Kissinger
17. *Pentagon Papers*
18. *Swann* v. *Charlotte-Mecklenburg Board of Education*
19. *Bakke* v. *Board of Regents of California*
20. Twenty-sixth Amendment
21. Spiro Agnew
22. OPEC
23. SALT
24. détente
25. George McGovern
26. Watergate
27. Saturday Night Massacre
28. War Powers Act
29. Camp David Accords

VOCABULARY BUILDING

Listed below are some words used in this chapter. Look in the dictionary for the meaning of each.

1. elusive
2. seismic
3. hierarchical
4. precipitate
5. coalesce

6. nihilistic
7. pacifist
8. disaffected
9. credo
10. karma
11. tout
12. bastion
13. restitution
14. fractious
15. assuage
16. ignoble
17. tandem
18. malaise
19. deranged
20. complicity
21. melodrama
22. resiliency
23. perplex
24. unconscionable
25. rapprochement
26. depraved
27. interregnum
28. amnesty
29. barrage
30. epitomize

EXERCISES FOR UNDERSTANDING

When you have completed reading the chapter, answer each of the following questions. If you have difficulty, go back and reread the section of the chapter related to the question.

Multiple-Choice Questions

Select the letter of the response that best completes the statement.

1. "Participatory democracy" was a slogan common in the
   A. Kennedy administration.
   B. counterculture.
   C. New Left.
   D. National Organization for Women.
2. Divisions within American society reached a climax in 1968 at
   A. the Woodstock Music Festival.
   B. Columbia University in New York City.

C. the University of California with the Free Speech Movement.

D. the Democratic convention in Chicago.

3. The modern feminist movement was launched by
   A. the Port Huron Statement.
   B. Dr. Spock's *Baby and Child Care*.
   C. *The Feminine Mystique*.
   D. Timothy Leary.

4. In *Roe* v. *Wade*, the Supreme Court ruled
   A. all abortions constitutional.
   B. abortions constitutional in the first three months of pregnancy.
   C. all abortions unconstitutional.
   D. that only abortions for unmarried women were legal.

5. The United Farm Workers in the 1960s led a boycott of
   A. tobacco products.
   B. John Deere farm equipment.
   C. grapes.
   D. the AFL-CIO.

6. The raid at the Stonewall Inn in 1969 touched off the
   A. gay rights movement.
   B. right-to-life movement.
   C. Watergate scandal.
   D. antiwar movement.

7. Nixon's program to Vietnamize the Vietnam war meant
   A. restricting the fighting to South Vietnam.
   B. forcing the Chinese and Russians to stay out of the war.
   C. making the South Vietnamese do most of the fighting.
   D. all of the above

8. The last United States combat troops left Vietnam in
   A. June 1972.
   B. March 1973.
   C. August 1974.
   D. April 1975.

9. The Supreme Court endorsed busing to achieve school integration in
   A. *Brown* v. *Board of Education*.
   B. *Alexander* v. *Holmes County Board of Education*.
   C. *Bakke* v. *Board of Regents of California*.
   D. *Swann* v. *Charlotte Mecklenburg Board of Education*.

10. Stagflation was a new economic term for
    A. deflation and recession.
    B. inflation and depression.
    C. inflation and recession.
    D. deflation in part of the economy and inflation in the other part.

11. Causes of stagflation included
    A. rising oil prices.
    B. an expanding labor market.
    C. large federal deficits.
    D. all of the above

12. Henry Kissinger conducted "shuttle diplomacy" to create peace between
    A. the United States and the Soviet Union.
    B. Egypt and Israel.
    C. China and the Soviet Union.
    D. the United States and Vietnam.

13. Results of Watergate included the
    A. War Powers Act.
    B. creation of the imperial presidency.
    C. end of the war in Vietnam.
    D. all of the above

14. The Camp David Accords of 1978 were a peace agreement between
    A. the Soviet Union and the United States
    B. Vietnam and the United States.
    C. Britain and Ireland.
    D. Israel and Egypt.

15. As president, Jimmy Carter's biggest failure was in his handling of the
    A. economy.
    B. Iranian hostage crisis.
    C. Soviet invasion of Afghanistan.
    D. negotiations with the Soviet Union over nuclear weapons.

True-False Questions

Indicate whether each statement is true or false.

1. The Free Speech Movement began at the University of Michigan.
2. Hippies were part of the counterculture.
3. The Equal Rights Amendment was ratified in 1975.

4. By 1976 half of all married women were employed outside the home.
5. The founder of the United Farm Workers was Dennis Banks.
6. The maximum number of United States troops in Vietnam was 540,000 in 1969.
7. Four students were killed by National Guardsmen after antiwar rioting at Kent State University.
8. The greatest outcry against Nixon's Vietnam policy came after the Christmas bombings of 1972.
9. The Twenty-sixth Amendment gave eighteen-year olds the right to vote.
10. The Environmental Protection Act was passed during the Nixon administration.
11. The "Saturday Night Massacre" resulted from a battle over the best methods to deal with stagflation.
12. Richard Nixon was impeached.
13. Gerald Ford was elected vice president in 1972 and succeeded Nixon in 1974.
14. President Carter reached an agreement to turn the Panama Canal over to Panama.
15. The Iranian hostage crisis began a few days after the former shah of Iran entered the United States for medical treatment.

Essay Questions

1. How did the New Left and the counter-culture differ? In what ways were they similar?
2. How did the civil rights movement affect women, Chicanos, homosexuals, and Indians?
3. What was Nixon's Vietnam policy and was it successful?
4. Discuss the impact of the Vietnam War on American society.
5. How did Nixon try to appeal to the "silent majority" with his domestic policies? Did he succeed?
6. How important were Nixon's diplomatic achievements with China and the Soviet Union? Could a Democrat have achieved the same gains? Explain.
7. What were the major events in the Watergate crisis?
8. Of the three presidents in the 1970s (Nixon, Ford, and Carter), which was the most successful and which the least successful? Justify your answers.

ANSWERS TO MULTIPLE-CHOICE AND TRUE-FALSE QUESTIONS

Multiple-Choice Questions

1-C, 2-D, 3-C, 4-B, 5-C, 6-A, 7-C, 8-B, 9-D, 10-C, 11-D, 12-B, 13-A, 14-D, 15-A

True-False Questions

1-F, 2-T, 3-F, 4-T, 5-F, 6-T, 7-T, 8-F, 9-T, 10-T, 11-F, 12-F, 13-F, 14-T, 15-T

35

CONSERVATIVE INSURGENCY

CHAPTER OBJECTIVES

After you complete the reading and study of this chapter, you should be able to

1. Explain the popular appeal of Ronald Reagan.
2. Evaluate Ronald Reagan's economic policies.
3. Understand why commentators perceived the Reagan-Bush years as self-interested and greedy.
4. Discuss the U.S. role in Central America in the 1980s.
5. Assess the Iran-Contra affair.
6. Explain the economic difficulties of the Reagan-Bush era.
7. Describe the decline of communism in Europe in the late 1980s.
8. Discuss the causes and events of the Gulf War.

CHAPTER OUTLINE

I. Election of Reagan
  A. End of Carter administration
  B. Reagan's appeal
    1. Personality
    2. "Revolution of ideas"

  C. Background in the 1970s
    1. Demographic changes
      a. Older population
      b. Growth of Sunbelt
    2. Religious revival
      a. Fundamentalism
      b. "Moral Majority"
      c. Traditional values
    3. Backlash against feminism
      a. Phyllis Schlafly and anti-ERA movement
      b. Anti-abortion movement
  D. Election of 1980
    1. Reagan victory
    2. Voter apathy
    3. Democrats' declining appeal

II. Reagan's first term
  A. Reaganomics
    1. "Government is the problem"
    2. Tax cuts
    3. Budget deficits
    4. Expenditures slashed
    5. Recession
    6. 1982 tax increase
  B. "Teflon Presidency"
    1. Conflicts of interests
    2. Unethical behavior
    3. Reagan untouched
  C. Effects of social policies

      1. Labor unions

      2. Feminism

      3. Minorities

   D. Foreign affairs in the 1980s

      1. Reagan's anti-communism

      2. Military buildup

         a. "Star Wars"

         b. Rhetorical protests

      3. Emphasis on Central America

         a. El Salvador

         b. Nicaragua

            i. Sandinistas

            ii. Contras

      4. Middle East

         a. Iran-Iraq war

         b. Lebanon, PLO, Israel

      5. Grenada

III. Reagan's second term

   A. Election of 1984

      1. Economic recovery

      2. Mondale and taxes

   B. Domestic challenges

   C. Arms control talks

      1. Geneva negotiations

      2. Collapse at Iceland

   D. Decline in Reagan's popularity

      1. 1986 elections

      2. Revelations of "Irangate"

   E. Iran-Contra scandal

      1. Arms for hostages

      2. Profits to Contras

      3. North, Poindexter, McFarlane, Casey

      4. Tower Commission

      5. Special prosecutor and indictments

   F. Economic difficulties

      1. Soaring debt

      2. Stock market collapse

      3. Deficit reduction

   G. The left-out

      1. Homeless

         a. Low-cost housing shortage

         b. Gentrification

         c. Deinstitutionalization

      2. AIDS sufferers

   H. INF agreement

  I. Reagan legacy

      1. Welfare state intact

      2. Larger federal budget

      3. Hope restored

      4. Peacetime prosperity

      5. Democrats on defensive

      6. Larger gap between rich and poor

      7. Huge budget deficits

  J. 1988 election

      1. Michael Dukakis

      2. George Bush

      3. Mudslinging

      4. Results

IV. The Bush years

   A. Tone of the Bush administration

   B. Domestic policies

      1. Economic problems

         a. Savings and loan crisis

         b. Budget deficits

         c. Tax increases and spending cuts

      2. War on drugs

   C. Democratic movements in the world

      1. Tiananmen Square

      2. Gorbachev's politics

         a. Afghanistan

         b. Eastern Europe

         c. East Germany

      3. Chile

      4. Soviet Union

         a. Coup

         b. Boris Yeltsin

         c. Dissolution of Soviet Union

         d. Weapons reductions

      5. Panama

         a. Manuel Noriega and drugs

         b. U.S. invasion

         c. Surrender of Noriega

   D. The Gulf War

      1. Iraq invades Kuwait

      2. U.N. resolutions

      3. Desert Shield

      4. Congressional debate

      5. Desert Storm

      6. Cease-fire

      7. Saddam Hussein still in power

KEY ITEMS OF CHRONOLOGY

Reagan presidency	1981–1989
Economic Recovery Tax Act	August 1981
Attack on U.S. Marines in Beirut	October 1983
Invasion of Grenada	October 1983
Tax Reform Act	September 1986
Stock Market plunge	October 1987
INF Treaty	December 1987
Tiananmen Square demonstrations	June 1989
Fall of the Berlin Wall	November 1989
Iraq invades Kuwait	August 1990
Operation Desert Storm	January–February 1991
Parts of former Soviet Union become Commonwealth of Independent States	December 1991

TERMS TO MASTER

Listed below are some important terms or people with which you should be familiar after you complete the study of this chapter. Identify or explain each.

1. sunbelt
2. "Moral Majority"
3. Phyllis Schlafly
4. Reaganomics
5. capital gains tax
6. "Teflon Presidency"
7. Sandra Day O'Connor
8. Strategic Defense Initiative
9. Contras
10. Grenada
11. Walter Mondale
12. Iran-Contra affair
13. Lieutenant-Colonel Oliver North
14. Tower Commission
15. gentrification
16. AIDS
17. junk bonds
18. Tiananmen Square
19. *perestroika*
20. *glasnost*
21. Mikhail Gorbachev
22. Boris Yeltsin
23. the Gulf War
24. OPEC
25. Saddam Hussein
26. Desert Shield
27. Desert Storm

VOCABULARY BUILDING

Listed below are some words used in this chapter. Look in the dictionary for the meaning of each.

1. hobble
2. unabated
3. indignant
4. founder (v.)
5. dour
6. bloated
7. pagan
8. resounding
9. euphemism
10. impropriety
11. celestial
12. martial
13. strident
14. impede
15. tinderbox
16. eclipse
17. debacle
18. acclaim
19. offing
20. buffet (v.)
21. reverberate
22. calamitous

23. blighted
24. epochal
25. legacy
26. onslaught
27. interdiction
28. dissolution
29. apartheid
30. cabal

EXERCISES FOR UNDERSTANDING

When you have completed reading the chapter, answer each of the following questions. If you have difficulty, go back and reread the section of the chapter related to the question.

Multiple-Choice Questions

Select the letter of the response that best completes the statement.

1. Demographic forces favorable to Reagan and conservatism included growth in the
   A. young adult population.
   B. Sunbelt population.
   C. working-class population in the urban Northeast.
   D. number of immigrants from Latin America.
2. Reaganomics did *not* include
   A. cutting taxes.
   B. increasing defense spending.
   C. balancing the budget.
   D. reducing regulation of business.
3. The Economic Recovery Tax Act of 1981
   A. increased the tax on capital gains.
   B. cut personal income taxes by 25 percent.
   C. raised the maximum personal tax rate for the wealthy.
   D. all of the above
4. The term "Teflon Presidency" referred to Reagan's
   A. background in merchandising.
   B. ability to handle hot issues.
   C. avoidance of responsibility for scandals.
   D. reputation as a gourmet chef.
5. With the Strategic Defense Initiative, Reagan

A. provided defensive military aid to U.S. allies.
B. dramatically reduced defense spending.
C. achieved nuclear disarmament.
D. escalated the nuclear arms race.

6. Reagan saw the most serious communist threat in
   A. eastern Europe.
   B. the Middle East.
   C. Central America.
   D. southeast Asia.
7. In Nicaragua, the Reagan administration backed
   A. the Sandinistas.
   B. José Napoleón Duarte.
   C. the Contras.
   D. the PLO.
8. The Reagan Doctrine called for
   A. supporting anti-communist forces in the world.
   B. lowering tariff barriers.
   C. forcing OPEC to lower the price of crude oil.
   D. reducing nuclear weaponry.
9. The Iran-Contra affair involved
   A. selling arms for hostages in Iran.
   B. Lieutenant-Colonel Oliver North.
   C. secretly supporting rebels in Nicaragua.
   D. all of the above
10. In 1987, Reagan signed a treaty with Gorbachev
    A. restricting biological and chemical warfare.
    B. eliminating intermediate-range nuclear weapons.
    C. ending the controversy over Afghanistan.
    D. settling the dispute between Israel and Lebanon.
11. "Read my lips: *no new taxes*," said
    A. Ronald Reagan.
    B. Walter Mondale.
    C. Michael Dukakis.
    D. George Bush.
12. The most spectacular event in the collapse of the Soviet empire was the
    A. demonstration in Tiananmen Square.
    B. successful uprising in Romania.
    C. fall of the Berlin Wall.
    D. overthrow of Augusto Pinochet.

13. Under President Bush, the United States decided to
    A. withdraw many military personnel from Europe and Asia.
    B. destroy tactical nuclear weapons in Europe and Asia.
    C. take long-range bombers off 24-hour alert status.
    D. all of the above
14. To seize Manuel Noriega, President Bush sent the military into
    A. Chile.
    B. El Salvador.
    C. Panama.
    D. Grenada.
15. Desert Shield was a military operation to protect
    A. Israel.
    B. Kuwait.
    C. Iraq.
    D. Saudi Arabia.

True-False Questions

Indicate whether each statement is true or false.

1. Phyllis Schlafly was a leader in the backlash against feminism.
2. In 1980, Reagan won the votes of a majority of the eligible voters.
3. By 1983 the Reagan administration had piled up debts larger than all his predecessors combined.
4. In 1982, Reagan supported another reduction in taxes.
5. Sandra Day O'Connor was the first female justice on the Supreme Court.
6. In El Salvador, the United States backed José Napoleón Duarte.
7. In 1983, the United States sent soldiers to evacuate American medical students from Lebanon.
8. The Tower Commission endorsed the activities of Oliver North.
9. When Reagan left the presidency, the federal budget as a percentage of the gross domestic product was higher than when he entered the office.
10. Rescuing the savings and loan institutions cost taxpayers $500 billion.
11. Germany was finally reunified in 1990.
12. The end of apartheid in South Africa came under the presidency of Nelson Mandela.
13. More than twenty nations joined the United States in Desert Storm.
14. Desert Storm was aimed against Iran.
15. In Desert Storm, the United States lost 1,375 soldiers and airmen.

Essay Questions

1. Were the 1980s most like the Gilded Age, the 1920s, or the 1950s? Why?
2. How did the Reagan-Bush economic policies affect Americans? Which were helped the most and which the least? Why?
3. What actions did Reagan and Bush take in Central America?
4. What was the Iran-Contra affair? Explain its significance.
5. How did U.S.-Soviet relations changes in the 1980s and 1990s?
6. Why and how did the United States get involved in the Gulf War in 1990–1991?

ANSWERS TO MULTIPLE-CHOICE AND TRUE-FALSE QUESTIONS

Multiple-Choice Questions

1-B, 2-C, 3-B, 4-C, 5-D, 6-C, 7-C, 8-A, 9-D, 10-D, 11-B, 12-C, 13-D, 14-D, 15-D

True-False Questions

1-T, 2-F, 3-T, 4-F, 5-T, 6-T, 7-F, 8-F, 9-T, 10-T, 11-T, 12-F, 13-T, 14-F, 15-F

36 ∽

CULTURAL POLITICS

CHAPTER OBJECTIVES

After you complete the reading and study of this chapter, you should be able to

1. Understand the demographic and technical changes affecting the nation in the 1990s.
2. Explain the impact of cultural and political conservatives under Bush and Clinton.
3. Evaluate the domestic programs of the Clinton administration.
4. Describe the economic and social trends of the 1990s.
5. Assess the foreign policies of the United States after the end of the cold war.
6. Appreciate the mood of the nation at the turn of the millennium.

CHAPTER OUTLINE

I. The nation in the 1990s
   A. Demographic changes
      1. Aging population
      2. Growth of Sunbelt
      3. Metropolitan growth
      4. Working women
      5. Decline of family unit
      6. African-American poverty

   B. New immigrants
      1. Non-European
      2. Resurgent nativism
   C. Computer revolution
      1. First-generation computers
      2. Postwar developments
         a. Private corporations
         b. The transistor
      3. Third generation
         a. Microprocessor
         b. Personal computer
         c. Bill Gates
      4. Internet

II. Cultural conservatism
   A. Attack on liberalism
      1. Against "political correctness"
      2. Against affirmative action
   B. Religious right
      1. Christian Coalition
      2. Political activism

III. Bush to Clinton
   A. Background to 1992 election
      1. Disruptions in foreign policy
         a. Gulf War
         b. Collapse of the Soviet Union
      2. Recession and unemployment
         a. Increasing joblessness
         b. Layoffs of white-collar workers

3. Nomination of Clarence Thomas
   a. Thomas's conservatism
   b. Charges of Anita Hill
   c. Senate hearings
   d. Gender gap
B. Republican problems
   1. Tax increases
   2. Christian Right and divisions
C. Election of 1992
   1. Background of Bill Clinton
      a. Governor of Arkansas
      b. Moderate
      c. "Slick Willie"
   2. Results

IV. Clinton's first administration
A. Economic policies
   1. Deficit reduction
   2. NAFTA
B. Health care reform
   1. Precedents
   2. Opposition
   3. Defeat
C. Militia movement
   1. Anti-government
   2. Waco, Texas
   3. Oklahoma City

V. Republican insurgency
A. Election of 1994
   1. Republican control of Congress
   2. Repudiation of Clinton
   3. Clinton's reaction
B. Contract with America
   1. Newt Gingrich
   2. Ten-point contract
   3. Congressional action
   4. Results
   5. Clinton moves to center
C. Legislative breakthroughs in 1996
   1. Increments in minimum wage and health care
   2. Welfare reform
D. 1996 election
   1. Bob Dole
   2. Results

VI. Economic and social trends in Clinton's second term
A. The economy
   1. Prosperity
   2. Budget surplus
   3. Alan Greenspan
   4. Globalization
B. The courts and race
   1. Gerrymandering
   2. "Reverse discrimination"
   3. Affirmative action
C. Scandals
   1. Whitewater
   2. Allegations of sexual impropriety
   3. Kenneth Starr's report
   4. Impeachment of Clinton
      a. Charges
         i. Lying under oath
         ii. Obstruction of justice
      b. Senate trial
      c. Acquittal

VII. Foreign Affairs
A. Low priority
B. Somalia
C. Haiti
   1. Support for Aristide
   2. Negotiations and troops
D. Middle East
   1. Inclusion of PLO in talks
   2. Israel-PLO agreement
   3. Assassination of Rabin
   4. 1998 agreement among Arafat, Hussein, and Netanyahu
E. Yugoslavia
   1. Ethnic conflict
   2. Peace plan
   3. Kosovo
      a. 1998 flare-up
      b. Ethnic cleansing
      c. NATO air strikes

VIII. America at the end of the century
A. Conflicting attitudes
   1. Celebration of prosperity
   2. Anxiety and doubt
B. Threats to cohesion and consensus
   1. Multicultural tensions
   2. Divisive issues and discourse

KEY ITEMS OF CHRONOLOGY

Invention of the transistor	1947
Invention of microprocessor	1971
First personal computer	1975
End of the Soviet Union	December 25, 1991
Clarence Thomas controversy	1991
Inauguration of Bill Clinton	January 20, 1993
Family Leave Act	February 1993
Siege at Waco, Texas	February–April 1993
Brady Bill passed	1993
Israel-PLO agreement	September 13, 1993
NAFTA passed by Congress	November 1993
Troops land in Haiti	September 19, 1994
Kenneth Starr named independent counsel	1994
Republican landslide	November 1994
Contract with America	1995
Oklahoma City bombing	April 1995
Personal Responsibility and Work Opportunity Act	1996
Hopwood v. *Texas*	1996
Federal budget surplus	1998–1999
Clinton impeached	December 1998
Clinton acquitted	February 1999
NATO air strikes in Kosovo begin	March 1999

TERMS TO MASTER

Listed below are some important terms or people with which you should be familiar after you complete the study of this chapter. Identify and explain each name or term.

1. Christian Coalition
2. downsizing
3. Clarence Thomas
4. NAFTA
5. militia movement
6. Contract with America
7. Newt Gingrich
8. Personal Responsibility and Work Opportunity Act
9. Robert Dole
10. Alan Greenspan
11. globalization
12. affirmative action
13. *Hopwood* v. *Texas*
14. Kenneth Starr
15. Whitewater
16. *ad hoc*
17. Kosovo
18. ethnic cleansing
19. *fin-de-siècle*

VOCABULARY BUILDING

Listed below are some words used in this chapter. Look up each word in the dictionary.

1. maturation
2. postindustrial
3. homicide
4. bilingual
5. disproportionate
6. prototype
7. facilitate
8. dogmatic
9. libertarian
10. abhor

11. resurgent
12. euphoria
13. disarray
14. pander
15. salacious
16. apocalyptic
17. incense (v.)
18. decimate
19. galvanize
20. ballyhoo (v.)
21. tout
22. abdicate
23. acerbic
24. monetarist
25. recant
26. amok
27. juncture
28. implode
29. retribution
30. seductive

EXERCISES FOR UNDERSTANDING

When you have completed reading the chapter, answer each of the following questions. If you have difficulty, go back and reread the section of the chapter related to the question.

Multiple-Choice Questions

Select the letter of the response that best completes the statement.

1. Demographic changes in the 1980s and 1990s included
   A. movement to the Midwest and Northeast.
   B. aging of the baby-boom generation.
   C. a return to rural America.
   D. all of the above
2. Out of a total population of 275 million in 2000, the number of farmers amounted to only
   A. 200,000.
   B. 2 million.
   C. 10 million.
   D. 20 million.
3. Immigration to the United States in the 1990s was
   A. mostly from Europe.
   B. at an all-time low.
   C. at an all-time high.
   D. typical of the post-World War II era.
4. ENIAC, the first computer, appeared in
   A. 1944.
   B. 1953.
   C. 1962.
   D. 1971.
5. The religious right included
   A. evangelical Christians.
   B. Jerry Falwell and Pat Robertson.
   C. the Christian Coalition.
   D. all of the above
6. The president during Desert Storm was
   A. Ronald Reagan.
   B. George Bush.
   C. Robert Dole.
   D. Bill Clinton.
7. George Bush's reelection chances suffered most from the
   A. defeat in Desert Storm.
   B. economic recession.
   C. unexpected collapse of communism.
   D. rise of the Christian right.
8. The major issue in the confirmation hearings for Clarence Thomas was
   A. charges of sexual harassment.
   B. his service during the Vietnam War.
   C. allegations that he had falsified his income tax returns.
   D. suspicion that he was a homosexual.
9. The Contract with America included
   A. term limits for representatives.
   B. more aggressive conservation of natural resources.
   C. gun control legislation.
   D. a ban on prayer in the public schools.
10. In 1996 welfare reform
   A. halted federal funds for welfare.
   B. turned many of the major programs over to the states.
   C. required that everyone receiving welfare had to work.
   D. was defeated by the Republicans in Congress.

11. By 1999, the Dow Jones industrial average had reached a peak of
    A. 1,000.
    B. 6,000.
    C. 11,000.
    D. 121,000.
12. In the 1990s, the Supreme Court
    A. ruled against gerrymandering to insure minority officeholding.
    B. restricted affirmative action programs.
    C. limited actions to achieve school integration.
    D. all of the above
13. President Clinton was impeached for
    A. having "inappropriate intimate physical contact" with Monica Lewinsky.
    B. his fraudulent behavior in the Whitewater scandal.
    C. lying and obstructing justice.
    D. all of the above
14. In the Middle East, the Clinton administration sponsored new negotiations between
    A. Israel and Egypt.
    B. Lebanon and the PLO.
    C. Lebanon and Egypt.
    D. the PLO and Israel.
15. In 1995, President Clinton sent 20,000 troops to maintain peace in
    A. Somalia.
    B. Israel.
    C. the former Soviet Union.
    D. the former Yugoslavia.

True-False Questions

Indicate whether each statement is true or false.

1. The postindustrial economy involved more jobs in service industries.
2. By 2000, most children did not live with two parents.
3. The leading cause of death for black males between the ages of fifteen and twenty-four in 2000 was homicide.
4. The transistor was invented during World War II.
5. Cultural conservatives were especially bothered by affirmative action programs.
6. George Bush nominated Anita Hill for a seat on the Supreme Court.
7. Before becoming president, Bill Clinton had been governor of Arkansas.
8. The most important issue in the 1992 presidential election was the economy.
9. Negotiated by Bush and backed by Clinton, NAFTA made North America a free-trade area.
10. Militia members were responsible for the Oklahoma City bombing in 1995.
11. In the 1996 elections, the Democrats won the presidency and control of Congress.
12. Industrial outsourcing contributed to the growing strength of American labor unions.
13. The Whitewater scandal involved a real estate deal in Arkansas.
14. President Clinton continued the Bush administration's policies in Somalia and the Middle East.
15. Dealing with multiple cultures within the nation was a major problem for the United States at the turn of the century.

Essay Questions

1. How did the demography of the United States change in the last two decades of the twentieth century? Why were the changes important?
2. Why was Bush defeated for reelection in 1992, and why did the Democrats stage a resurgence?
3. How did the foreign policies of the Bush and Clinton administrations differ? How were they similar?
4. What effects did cultural conservatives have on American society in the last years of the twentieth century?
5. How can the nation reconcile cultural pluralism and ethnic diversity with a national unity without ethnic conflict?
6. How was the United States different at the end of the century from what it had been at the end of World War II?

ANSWERS TO MULTIPLE-CHOICE AND TRUE-FALSE QUESTIONS

Multiple-Choice Questions

1-B, 2-B, 3-C, 4-A, 5-D, 6-B, 7-B, 8-A, 9-A, 10-B, 11-C, 12-D, 13-C, 14-D, 15-C

True-False Questions

1-T, 2-F, 3-T, 4-F, 5-T, 6-F, 7-T, 8-T, 9-T, 10-T, 11-F, 12-F, 13-T, 14-T, 15-T